Deliver Great
Training Courses
In A Week

WITHDRAWN

Martin Manser is an expert communicator with a unique combination of skills and experience. He has compiled or edited over 200 reference books on the English language, Bible reference and business skills in a 30-year professional career. He is an English-language specialist and teaches English to business colleagues: participants in his courses find them to be a safe place to ask questions and for participants' confidence to grow.

Since 2002 Martin has also been a Language Consultant and Trainer, leading training courses in business communications for national and international companies and organizations on language learning, report writing, project management and time management.

www.martinmanser.co.uk

I wish to thank Jean Howlett for her careful typing of my manuscript and Antonia Maxwell for her thorough checking of my text.

Deliver Great Training Courses In A Week

Martin Manser

**Also available
in ebook**

Contents

Introduction

You have probably been on both good and bad training courses. Unfortunately, it may be the bad ones that you remember – perhaps the content was badly ordered, the arrangements were poor, the speaker was boring. How can you prepare for and lead an outstanding training course? In this book we will show you how as you explore the following:

Sunday: What is training? What are you aiming to achieve? What are the basic different styles in which colleagues learn – and in which trainers train? What overall points should you consider and what practical arrangements do you need to think about, for example on timing and venue?

Monday: Identify the training needs clearly How to analyse participants' training needs, using various sources; use the needs to define clear learning outcomes that are both SMART and also relevant to participants' real work and jobs.

Tuesday: Design the course carefully How to continue to prepare well: think about the points you want to communicate and order them clearly; find a fresh angle; be motivational, inspirational and practical; write a strong beginning and round off your training well at the end.

Wednesday: Plan variety creatively Why the need to change the style of training regularly throughout the session is important to maintain participants' interest and involvement; plan variety; consider different ways to encourage group participation; use visual aids and PowerPoints effectively.

Thursday: Implement your plan successfully Go for it! Put all your preparation into practice on the day itself. How will you make a good first impression and make the most of informal times? Body language is important; how will you overcome nerves? Learn how to deal with difficult people.

Friday: Evaluate the training thoroughly Why identifying what went well and what didn't go so well is important; checking on 'learning' after the course is essential to determine changed attitudes, behaviour patterns, and so on. Review your training to see if it had its desired effects: if not, reassess and begin the process again.

Saturday: Refine your skills constantly You have completed your training course and evaluated it; now learn how to cultivate the qualities of a professional trainer, for example by keeping up to date with your subject, learning from your mistakes and mentoring a colleague to lead training courses.

Each day of the week covers a different area, and the material is structured by beginning with an introduction as to what the day is about. Then comes the main material which explains the key lessons by clarifying important principles that are backed up by tips, case studies and so on. Each day concludes with a summary, follow-up exercise and multiple-choice questions, to reinforce the learning points. Finally, at the end of the book is a new '7 × 7' section that offers a distillation of the guidance given in this book, together with some inspirational quotes and resources.

The principles I outline here are the fruit of over 30 years in business, particularly in the area of communications, and over 12 years in leading courses on business communications. As I have reflected on participants' responses to the training courses I have led, two comments keep recurring: 'You gave me more confidence' and 'Today was a refresher course.' My hope therefore is that as you read and act on what I have written, it will be a refresher course that will give you fresh confidence to lead and organize training courses.

Martin Manser

SUNDAY

What is training?

At the end of last week, your boss suggested that you should think about organizing some training courses for colleagues. Since then you have spent the weekend becoming enthusiastic about everything you can do. You are now ready to put all your plans energetically into action.

But where do you start? Arranging speakers? Booking venues? This chapter is designed to help you channel your energy and enthusiasm effectively and begin to lay a firm foundation for your training.

Today we will look at some basic questions:

- What are you aiming to achieve?
- How do people learn?
- What are the best ways of enabling colleagues to learn? What about online courses?
- How do people train?
- Should you use an internal or external trainer?
- What areas, broadly speaking, do you want the training to cover?
- What practical points do you need to consider?

Some basic questions

In your preparation as you consider training, you should ask yourself the following questions:

- **Who?**
  - Who needs training? For example, certain individuals with particular needs or all colleagues with a certain role?
  - Who needs to be involved? Do you have all the necessary resources?
  - Who will lead the training, for example experts in the area, or yourself?
  - If you are an outside trainer or are using a particular venue, who is the contact person you will deal with? Ensure that you have their contact details.
  - Who will authorize the cost?
- **Why?**
  - Why is the training needed? What is its context in your company or organization?
  - Why are you leading, organizing or arranging the training? Consider your role: are you the best person to lead the actual training or would someone else be more suitable?
- **Where?**
  - Where will the training be held?
  - Where will you find suitable trainers, if you are not leading the actual training yourself?
- **When?**
  - When will you hold the training? Soon? In three months' time? Next year? How much notice do you need to give the venue where you are holding the training? How much notice do you need to give the participants and the speaker? (Throughout this book, I use the word 'participants', not 'delegates', because I want to emphasize 'participants' actively taking part in a training course rather than their merely attending.)
  - When will you put in place a timetable for all the arrangements that need to be made?

● How?

- How did the requirement for training arise: what is its context?
- How did this particular need fit into the overall aims of the learning and development programme of your company or organization?
- How are you going to train the colleagues concerned? What method(s) will you use? Will you hold a face-to-face training course or develop an online course or use a combination of both styles?
- How long will the training course be? Is there to be more than one course? Will the training take place over a number of days? If so, how many?
- How is the need for training to be presented? Will colleagues be told they have to go on the course or will they be persuaded over a period of time that this course would be very helpful to them?
- How will the training be presented? What visual aids, for example PowerPoint, will you need?
- How will any special needs of the participants be accommodated?
- How will the impact of the training on individuals or organizations be measured and evaluated?
- How will you know whether the training has been effective?
- How much will the training cost (and who is going to pay for it)?

● What?

- What is the purpose of the training?
- What, in broad terms, do you expect to be covered in the training?
- What is expected from the training? What do you want participants to be able to do as a result of the training?
- What is expected to happen after the training?

We will consider these throughout this book.

> ## Case study: Passing on what you have learned
>
> Colin felt tired. He knew his job well but had lost enthusiasm for it and had become rather dissatisfied with his company. He was surprised therefore when his boss suggested that he should train new colleagues. As Colin discussed this opportunity with friends, he realized that he had not only a lot of knowledge but also specific skills that he could pass on to new colleagues. In short, his experience was invaluable.
>
> He realized, however, that he required a refresher course in training and communication, so he attended an external 'Train the Trainer' course. After completing that course and as he began to train new members of staff, he suddenly sensed a fresh and positive energy in his new role.

What are you aiming to achieve?

Different training courses have different aims so it is important to be aware of what you want to achieve. Possible aims include:

- communicating a quantity of information on a subject
- communicating an understanding of a subject, so that participants can apply the knowledge gained
- communicating a skill so that participants' behaviour will be changed: by the end of the course they will be able to do something they could not do before
- designing a refresher course that aims to fill in gaps in participants' knowledge
- increasing participants' confidence.

For example, I am a poor swimmer. I could receive information on breathing techniques and different swimming strokes in a workshop but that would be different from actually going to a swimming pool, getting wet and putting what I had heard into practice. Similarly, a training course in first aid would not only discuss different techniques theoretically but also give the participants the practical skills to act in certain situations.

For me the delight in being a trainer is in:

- creating a relaxed atmosphere in which participants can ask questions and learn easily
- seeing individuals make significant steps forward as they understand something for the first time
- seeing participants apply what they have learned when they return to their ordinary work.

I remember meeting a participant from one of my time-management courses three months after the course. He came up to me beaming. 'I've put into practice all the lessons you taught us,' he told me, 'and I've almost caught up on all my work.'

For me, the ultimate aim in training is to see changed habits.

How do people learn?

Every individual is different, and if we want to train colleagues effectively, we would be wise to try to discover their preferred learning style. There are three main learning styles:

- **Visual** – those who like to see information in the written word, pictures, videos or diagrams to take it in well.
- **Auditory** – those who learn by listening to information.
- **Kinaesthetic** – those who learn by actively doing things, through role play or team games, for example.

It can be very useful for you to discern where your own personal preference lies: I am more visual and auditory rather than kinaesthetic. The aim here is to challenge your assumption that the way other people learn is the same as the way that you learn. You need this reminder that other people's learning styles will be different from yours. To be an effective trainer, you therefore need to be alert to the styles of those you want to train.

You can discern others' style from how they respond and you can then use these words as indicators of their style. Here are some examples:

- **Visual:** see, look, picture, focus.
- **Auditory:** hear ('I hear what you're saying'), buzz, rings a bell
- **Kinaesthetic:** feel, concrete, get to grips with, contact.

The significance of this is that an effective training course will incorporate elements of all three: visual and auditory elements, for example written words on screens and pictures and/or diagrams to accompany them, as well as active discussion and role play to put ideas into action. (For active discussion, I find that putting participants in pairs is helpful, as one person's weaknesses may balance out another person's strengths.)

Case study: A variety of styles

Jim had almost completed a day course with a small group of colleagues when one told him that she learned most effectively by drawing diagrams of the steps she needed to take. Jim was a wordsmith and had falsely assumed that all the colleagues he was training were similar to him. So all of Jim's steps began with the same letter ('in communication, be **C**lear, **C**oncise, **C**orrect') or with a sequence of letters of the alphabet ('Be **A**ccurate, be **B**rief, be **C**lear').

From that day on, he was more aware of the range of different colleagues' learning styles and took steps to ensure that he included visual elements wherever possible, such as a picture of an arrow reaching the bull's eye of a target to demonstrate effective communication. He also often included role play: in a basic course on project management he would assign different roles to different participants, asking them to work through a range of aspects such as costing and scheduling for a particular project, for example building facilities for a future Olympic Games. In this way, his training became more rounded and effective.

On a course I led on writing, for all my words, what was most important for some colleagues was the following picture that demonstrated the approximate thirds taken up by different

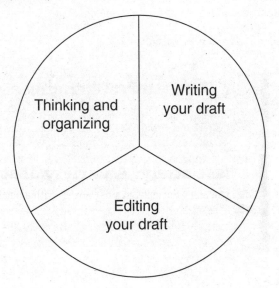

parts of the writing process. The sheer visual element made the greatest impact.

How do people train?

Alongside the different ways in which colleagues learn, you should also think of your own preferred training style. Of course, you may well have one style that comes more easily to you but, as we have just noted, you should take into account your participants' style, too. You should also adapt your personal style of training to the particular course you are leading.

The variety of training styles include:

- The trainer presents information in a straight **lecture style**: this is especially suitable for larger groups.
- The trainer leads in more of a **discussion style**: the trainer asks the participants questions (as a group, individuals, in pairs) to stimulate their thinking. The trainer then acts as more of a facilitator. (This is my preferred style as I work on the basis that participants will learn or benefit most from what they themselves have discussed or spoken

about rather than what I have told them and they have only heard. Of course, at times I also have to present information directly.)

- The trainer leads by using great involvement by the participants in **action/role play**.

> ## Case study: Changing styles
>
> Nick was a good trainer. He enjoyed asking questions of the participants who attended his courses. His colleague Daniel sat in on one of his workshops, however, and noticed that the participants weren't really participating. Daniel had a quiet word with Nick at the mid-morning break, telling him to 'do something' and change his style. Fortunately, Nick accepted David's advice and involved the participants in a small group activity and so the training course turned out well.

Online training?

Online training may be most suitable where you have a quantity of information that needs to be assimilated, for example on information management or certain health and safety regulations. Multiple-choice questions can then test users' knowledge.

However, I believe that the presence of trainer and participants being trained in one physical space is more conducive to effective learning, mainly because I believe the rapport between trainer and those being trained is significant. There will always be questions that the participants will (when they feel relaxed) ask a trainer while they are on the training course which I don't believe they would ask a computer.

It may well be that blended learning – a combination of online and face-to-face learning – is a possible way forward. Also coming into fashion are webinars (*web* + sem*inar*), which are interactive online workshops.

Using an internal or external trainer?

As a manager, you should consider which is the best way to develop your staff. Here are some examples of different ways of doing this:

- **On-the-job training:** this is directly relevant to individuals, but you need to find an effective trainer.
- **In-house training:** this is useful if your whole company or organization needs to develop certain knowledge or skills but may not be so relevant to particular individuals.
- **External training led by a professional expert, either at your office or at another venue:** there can be particular value in learning at a site that is away from your workplace. (If training is undertaken at your place of work, participants are more likely to be called out for meetings; an external venue lessens the likelihood of such a possibility.)

In looking for courses, consider:

- **the outcomes of the course:** what will your colleagues be able to do as a result of attending a particular course? We will discuss this further on Monday.
- **the flexibility of the course design:** if you are asking an external trainer to quote for fulfilling your particular training requirements, you will want to be sure that they will listen to your needs and design a course based on such needs, rather than just present a standard existing course. We will look more at course design on Tuesday.
- **the background and credentials of the trainers.**

After a training course it is important to have some form of evaluation to ensure that some of the principles 'learned' on the course have been digested and integrated into your participants' work practices. Remember: 'Use it or lose it' – apply what you have 'learned' or you will forget it. We will discuss this further on Friday.

'Use it or lose it – apply what you have learned or you will forget it.'

Case study: The benefits of an outside facilitator

Sarah was due to lead an in-house half-day training session on negotiation skills at Johnson & Company. She arrived early at the company's offices and was offered a cup of coffee by a member of staff who was to attend the course. Another member of staff's immediate response to the offer of a coffee was, 'Well, you never make me a cup of coffee!' Sarah immediately sensed tension in the organization. The course went very well, and she was commended for having enabled two different groups who didn't normally talk to each other to work together successfully.

Sometimes inviting an outside facilitator to lead a course in a company can achieve significantly more than a colleague within the company: the outside facilitator may become aware of issues that are overlooked in a company and may be able to speak into a situation more directly because they are not involved in any internal politics.

Case study: On-the-job training

For several weeks Rose was seconded one afternoon a week to help Joanne, a new team member, learn how to use the new software. First of all, Rose explained to Joanne how to operate a different aspect of the software as she (Rose) actually performed the task. Then Rose got Joanne to do it, and Rose repeated parts of the explanation that were not clear to Joanne. Finally, Joanne both did and explained what she was doing to Rose, who was delighted with the results. Using a step-by-step showing-and-telling method, Joanne had quickly learned how to use the software by herself.

Coaching and mentoring

Coaching and mentoring can work alongside training as more personal and direct ways of developing a colleague and their skills. The differences could be summed up as:

Coaching	Mentoring
More short-term	Often more long-term
More formal and structured	More informal
Is directed at specific issues or the development of specific skill areas	Considers the person as a whole and provides guidance in career development
Could be your line manager or even a colleague on the same level as you but with more experience	Undertaken by an individual higher up in your company or organization (but *not* your boss) or even someone from a different organization

A good coach or mentor:

- will be good at listening to what the person being coached is saying and not saying. They will be able to 'read (and listen) between the lines' and ask good questions
- will not always respond with answers but will encourage the person being coached to actively come up with solutions to difficulties. Colleagues are more likely to act on them if they

have worked through the issues for themselves than if a coach has simply provided an answer
● will bring a different way of thinking about an issue or a problem as they seek to understand that issue or problem.

Case study: Discussing aspirations with a mentor

Maria met regularly with Janet, her mentor. Janet wasn't Maria's line manager, so Maria felt able to discuss her work freely and confidentially with Janet. In particular, Maria was able to talk through her aspirations. The mentoring sessions included discussion of Maria's short- and mid-term training needs, and after the mentoring sessions Maria was able to approach her line manager to discuss these with her.

Over time, the combination of 'evolution' – small changes that Maria introduced into her working practices – and 'revolution' – lessons learned on training courses – proved very beneficial to Maria's career.

Consider practical arrangements

As part of your preparation, you need to consider practical aspects of the training. Again, answering of the question words can help you:

● **Why?**
   – Why do you need the training? What is its context in your company or organization? How has the need for training arisen? Have particular needs arisen from individual colleagues' performance reviews?
● **When?**
   – When will you hold the training? As necessary, check that the proposed dates do not clash with school holidays or other significant times, such as major religious holidays or national sports fixtures.
   – When will the training be on the day? Start times, finish times; times for breaks for mid-morning, lunch,

mid-afternoon? If such times are exact, then ask for refreshments to be available promptly: you do not want to wait for coffee for ten minutes in a 20-minute coffee break!

– When will you send out publicity for the course? What means will you use, for example email, mentions at regular meetings?

– When will the list of participants be finalized? If you are an outside trainer, it can be very helpful to have a list of names in advance so that you can see the number of participants who will attend and also, for example, how many men and how many women will be attending.

– When could you gain access to the room to finalize setting up any equipment? If possible, allow an hour, or at least 30 minutes, to do this: some participants might arrive early and ideally you would want to be available to talk to them rather than be involved in setting up equipment.

● **Where?**

– Where will you hold the training? In your offices? Book rooms as necessary. At an outside location? Check car parking facilities and/or access to public transport as necessary.

– If the training is to be held at an outside location, is the venue used to handling training courses? Who will deal with registration of participants? Will refreshments be

served on the arrival of the participants? If so, by whom? Who will bring the participants into the training room? What refreshments will be provided for breaks and lunch? Ensure that you are aware of all (especially any hidden) costs. If in doubt, ask.
- Ensure that all rooms, including toilets, are accessible for those with any disability.
- Discuss the style of any major meals, such as lunch; to save time, buffet-style self-service meals are best.
- Does the venue have facilities for last-minute photocopying? Hopefully, this would not be necessary, but it might be.
- What is the training room like? Consider its acoustics. Is the lighting adequate for your purposes? Natural light is best. Is the heating and/or air conditioning adequate (i.e. not too noisy)?
- Are there enough accessible sockets for a laptop, projector, and so on? Who would provide an extension lead?
- Will you need a microphone? If so, ensure that one is available.
- Check access to fire exits.
- What about seating arrangements? Try to avoid classroom style, except for large groups; horseshoe (u-shaped) seating works well, in that you as trainer can have good eye contact with all participants and they can also talk to one another. Cabaret/restaurant style seating can also work.
- Will you be able to stick papers, for example from flip charts, on the walls of the room?
- **Who?**
  - Who will lead the training sessions? Will you have an external trainer?
  - Will you invite special speakers? If the speaker is well known, you will want to use their name in publicity, so book that person as far in advance as possible.
  - Who needs training? Who do you want to come? Will colleagues be encouraged, persuaded or even told to come? (The more willing participants are to attend, the more receptive they are likely to be.)

- Specify dress code if there might be some doubt about this.
- Who will be responsible for providing laptop, projector, lead from laptop to projector screen, screen, flip chart, flip chart pens, name cards/badges, certificates of attendance?

● **How?**
- How will you decide what training methods to use? See earlier today on lecturer/facilitator styles.
- How much will the training cost? Have you set yourself a budget? If not, do one now. See below for an example.

Costs	
Speaker	4,000
Venue	6,000
Marketing	3,000
Administration	2,000
Office	2,000
Contingency	2,000
TOTAL	19,000
Income	
Participants' fees	22,000
Profit	**3,000**

- How will you evaluate the training course to know whether or not it has been effective?

● **What?**
- What will be the content of the training? See Monday, Tuesday and Wednesday for more on this.
- What follow-up and/or evaluation are you planning? See Friday.

Summary

Today we have begun to lay the foundation for effective training by undertaking careful preparation. You need to think through the following questions:

- **Why** do you want to have the training: what is the context in your company or organization?
- **What** will be the content of the course in broad terms? What are you hoping to achieve by the training?
- **Whom** do you want to be trained? Who will lead the training?
- **How** do you want the training to be undertaken: face-to-face or online or a combination of the two?
- **When** will you conduct the training? How soon? How long will the training course last?
- **Where** do you want the training to be held?
- **How** much will the training cost?

Follow-up

With reference to a current training course you are organizing, consider and make notes on the following:

1 What are your aims in undertaking the training?

2 Who needs training? Who will lead the training course?

3 What are the next practical steps you need to take to arrange the training?

4 What, in broad terms, do you want the training course to cover?

Tomorrow, Monday, we will look more closely as how to assess and plan what you want to get out of the training course.

MONDAY

TUESDAY

WEDNESDAY

THURSDAY

FRIDAY

SATURDAY

Fact-check

1. Before a training course, you should:
   a) Just get on with it as quickly as possible ❏
   b) Prepare well, considering the context of the training and identifying needs ❏
   c) Plan to explain all you know on a subject ❏
   d) Not do anything, but just improvise on the day ❏

2. For a training course to be run successfully, you need to:
   a) Prepare and plan for it in detail ❏
   b) Think about it a day in advance ❏
   c) Hope everything goes well with as little planning as possible ❏
   d) Prepare for it so much that it never actually takes place ❏

3. People learn:
   a) All in the same way ❏
   b) In the same way as you ❏
   c) In a range of different ways ❏
   d) The way that you tell them to ❏

4. Participants learn best when they are:
   a) Hungry ❏
   b) Nervous and stressed ❏
   c) Relaxed ❏
   d) Angry ❏

5. When planning a training course you need especially to consider:
   a) What they have learned on the subject so far in their career ❏
   b) What to eat for lunch ❏
   c) What their future career prospects might be ❏
   d) What you want people to do as a result of attending the course ❏

6. All trainers should:
   a) Follow one particular style ❏
   b) Be flexible and adapt their personal style of training to the particular course they are leading ❏
   c) Follow their own preferred style ❏
   d) Follow their boss's own preferred style ❏

7. If you are using an outside trainer, you should:
   a) Find out as much as you can about their credentials ❏
   b) Not bother to check their credentials ❏
   c) Expect to be disappointed ❏
   d) Expect to be just satisfied ❏

8. When considering the venue for a training course, which of the following are not important:
   a) The room's lighting and heating ❏
   b) The room's acoustics ❏
   c) The colour of the walls ❏
   d) External noise ❏

9. A budget for the training course is:
a) Nice to have, if you have the time ❑
b) A waste of time, as no one keeps to it ❑
c) A luxury ❑
d) Essential ❑

10. Evaluation at the end of the course is:
a) Unnecessary ❑
b) Vital and should be considered at the outset in the planning ❑
c) Helpful if you remember ❑
d) A waste of time ❑

MONDAY

TUESDAY

WEDNESDAY

THURSDAY

FRIDAY

SATURDAY

MONDAY

Identify the training needs clearly

You have begun to lay a foundation and are now eager to start to arrange training or to actually train your colleagues. However, before you begin, you need to stop and assess precisely what you want to do. You need to consider:

- the different areas that colleagues need training in
- the present level of colleagues' knowledge, skills and confidence in the areas that they need training in
- the ultimate level of knowledge, skills and confidence that you want your colleagues to have after they have attended the training course and applied what they have learned back in their jobs.

In other words, you cannot move directly into the actual training until you have thought carefully about the precise requirements and why the training is necessary.

So today we will consider:

- assessing colleagues' starting points and their needs
- specifying certain learning outcomes that are relevant to colleagues' work so that you can know later whether or not the training has been effective.

Assess the starting point

Let's take an example. Suppose you work in retail management and have appointed area managers for shops. The area managers should liaise with shop managers, but some of the area managers find this difficult and the system you have in place is not working. You think that training them will help, but you need to think about the present skills, knowledge, experience and attitudes of the area managers. Do they know what is expected of them?

Having given the matter close thought, you realize that the responsibilities of area managers should include:

● knowing the names of the shop managers; the area managers should introduce themselves and get to know the shop managers at a professional level
● being able to articulate clearly company policy and targets to their staff
● ensuring their staff know about the products they are selling and that they all 'believe' in the company
● managing, valuing and inspiring their staff and needing to support staff members who underperform sensitively
● ensuring that staff at whatever level know that they are valued
● knowing how to manage more complex personnel (human resources) matters that individual shop managers cannot handle
● knowing how to handle routine administrative tasks passed down from head office.

As you think about this even more carefully, you observe that:

● all area managers are too busy especially because they are travelling around the country to deal with crises rather than planning their visits more effectively
● some area managers find it difficult to relate to certain shop managers, because they are (1) not assertive enough and/or (2) have not had enough experience of that particular company
● some area managers are spending too much time with certain shop managers and are neglecting other shop managers in their area, who feel ignored.

Over an extended period of time, as manager you conduct further investigations to supplement your observations. You consider:

- appraisals of colleagues. In their formal yearly appraisals and performance reviews, the performance of colleagues since their last review is assessed. What has gone well? What evidence is there to demonstrate this? What future development needs are there that can be met by training?
- discussion with other colleagues, bosses, subordinates, for example in '360-degree' appraisals
- discussion at a senior level on the significant difficulties and inconsistencies between high-level plans and reality
- discussion with other stakeholders, both inside and outside your company or organization
- the background of the weaknesses in knowledge, skills, experience, attitudes, and so on, that have led to the need for training
- formal and informal responses from customers, both complaints and compliments.

You stand back even further and with other managers you consider still wider questions:

- Who needs training? Does every member of staff in the company or organization? All the colleagues at a certain level or only the ones who have difficulties? How will you choose who is to undergo the training? What criteria will you use to identify them?
- What previous knowledge and experience do the colleagues whom you have identified as needing training have so far?
- Is training in fact the best way of dealing with the difficulty? Would an open discussion as a team be a useful first step?

You also consider:

- the results of questionnaires and 'skills audits' which consider the skills and knowledge that your company or organization needs, revealing certain gaps and weaknesses
- the results of focus groups – small groups that meet to discuss a particular issue – to identify the skills necessary

to reach certain performance targets and discuss how such skills could be improved
- competitors' strengths on certain issues
- industry trends: what changes are there in the market or in your end users' lifestyles? How are you responding to such changes?

As you bring all these results together, you draw conclusions and realize that you initially need to focus on two main issues:

1 Time management skills: making more effective use of colleagues' time, especially so that they can plan more regular visits to all the shops in their area.
2 Communication skills: improving colleagues' listening skills, building stronger working relationships so that managers value their staff more, and increasing assertiveness.

You therefore decide to consider training in these two areas for certain colleagues. On balance, you decide against the 'sheep-dip' approach where you put all colleagues through certain training, regardless of whether or not they need it. (In fact, you later discover that it would have been helpful if you as manager had attended the course on time management, as the course raised issues that needed to be be dealt with throughout the company, not only at the level of area managers.)

You have now begun to identify certain needs. In our example, area managers need to gain:

- certain knowledge and experience, for example in connection with time management, setting priorities, planning visits to shops in the same area more effectively
- certain skills, for example improving listening skills, valuing and motivating staff, becoming more assertive (but being neither passive nor aggressive)
- certain attitudes, for example to be more positive and professional.

All this is only the first step in identifying training needs, but notice how different it is from your relatively vague initial thoughts. And you can now move on from this.

You have now begun the training cycle.

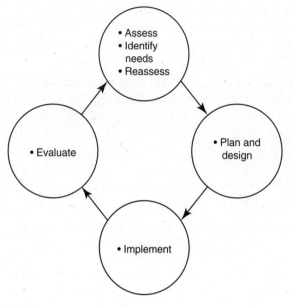

The training cycle

- **Assess:** identify training needs, for example in appraisals.
- **Plan and design:** having identified needs, you plan a training course.
- **Implement:** carry out the training course.
- **Evaluate:** review to see whether the training had its desired effects; if not, reassess and begin the process again; if it has, then you can identify a further area of development to work on a different course.

Specify certain learning outcomes

Having begun to assess where your colleagues are in a particular area of knowledge or skill and where you want them to be by the end of training, you now need to specify particular learning outcomes. If you do this, then when you evaluate the training after it has been completed, you will be in a position to know whether or not the learning has been effective.

There are two main criteria for considering learning outcomes:

1 **The learning outcomes should be relevant to your particular company or organization.** Some training is so general that it is left to the responsibility of the participants themselves to apply what has been discussed in the training to their work. In practice, however, participants may not always apply the training given and so it is wasted. So the outcomes should be relevant in a practical way to the jobs and work of the participants.

2 **The learning outcomes should be SMART:**
   - **S**pecific, defining the desired results.
   - **M**easurable, quantifiable so that you know whether the objectives have been reached.
   - **A**greed by all those concerned.
   - **R**ealistic: objectives that are achievable; not too easy but will develop and challenge ('stretch') colleagues' resources and skills.
   - **T**imed, giving a date for completion.

Some commentators add:
   - **E**valuated: progress on achieving SMART goals is reviewed at future meetings.
   - **R**eported: evaluated progress is reported and recorded.

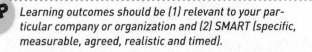

TIP *Learning outcomes should be (1) relevant to your particular company or organization and (2) SMART (specific, measurable, agreed, realistic and timed).*

Let's take a further example and consider an insurance company that writes reports on accidents. Here is an example of some learning outcomes for a writing course for colleagues working in such a company.

> *At the end of the course, participants will:*
>
> - *be able to write more effective documents*
> - *have greater confidence in working through the different stages of the writing process*
> - *know how to check documents so that they are clear and accurate*
> - *be familiar with how to deal with common problems of spelling, punctuation and usage.*

On the surface, these learning outcomes seem reasonable, but they may be deficient. Let's consider them in the light of the two criteria above.

1 **Are the learning outcomes relevant to the colleagues' actual work?** Yes, but only in a limited way. As you probe further, you discover that the area where colleagues really need help is knowing how to write about a complex subject in a clear and logical way. Currently, steps in an argument are sometimes omitted or repeated and the reports that colleagues write do not flow well. So a better learning outcome would be 'to write a complex argument in a clear and logical way'.

2 **Are the learning outcomes SMART?**
   - **Specific** – no: colleagues need help in writing about a complex subject clearly and logically, as just noted. A further area for development is that colleagues need to write emails in such a way that their tone is appropriate to the task; currently some customers have complained that the emails they receive are too abrupt. So a better learning outcome would be 'to write emails in an appropriate tone'.
   - **Measurable** – in a limited way. For example, 'confidence' could be subjective. If we had the revised learning outcomes of 'writing a complex argument in a clear logical way' and 'writing emails in an appropriate tone', then an objective measure would be that there would be fewer emails in response asking for clarification of the argument and fewer complaints commenting on the tone of the email.

31

- **Agreed** – yes.
- **Realistic** – yes, you want to challenge and stretch colleagues' abilities.
- **Timed** – no: the original learning objectives did not state any particular time, so that should now be added, for example 'within one month of the training'.

So, applying and extending our discussion on learning outcomes we could propose the following as learning outcomes:

Within a month of completing the course on writing, participants will be able to:

- *plan a document clearly*
- *write a complex argument in a clear and logical way*
- *write emails in a tone that is appropriate to the audience*
- *revise a document thoroughly*
- *use more active verbs, and fewer passive verbs*
- *spell words correctly*
- *use apostrophes, commas and hyphens correctly.*

Further points for learning outcomes

You should also consider the following points when writing learning outcomes:

- **Be realistic.** Keep to what you know you can do. You cannot change your whole company or organization overnight, but you can make significant changes in certain areas.
- **Consider the budget.** Here you may have the cost of a speaker, the venue and expenses of a speaker and participants. You may want to have a three-day course, but hotel expenses may be prohibitive for overnight stays for such a course so you will have to settle for a two-day one. (You could even start slightly later on the first day to allow participants time to travel in the early morning of the first

day of a two-day course. In this way you would incur costs only for one overnight stay, between the two days of the training.)

- **Involve other key individuals** as soon as you can. It is important that the training is not seen as the sole responsibility of you as training manager. As far as you can, involve other managers and/or colleagues in approving (signing off) training and, as appropriate, being present at the training, too.

Case study: Attitudes

Stuart led a two-day course. On the first day before mid-morning break there was no eye contact with any of the participants. He quickly realized that they were all angry at having been sent on the course. Stuart patiently listened to their complaints about being sent on the course, about their bosses and about the atmosphere at the company and its politics. Once the participants had expressed their emotions openly and fully during the first session on the first day, they were in a receptive mood to listen to what Stuart had to say. Stuart knew that initially the participants were resistant to his input, so initially this was minimal. Once the participants felt listened to, he could then, during the second session on the first day, begin the main part of his work. Stuart knew that attitudes, as well as knowledge, experience and skills, were also important.

Summary

Today we have laid a further level of foundation by identifying the needs of those you want to train. Specifically, we have considered:

- the present level and background in terms of knowledge, skills, attitude, and so on, of those you want to train
- the level in terms of knowledge, skills, attitude, and so on, that you want those being trained to have reached by the end of the training
- the identity of those you want to train and how you will choose them
- the learning outcomes: specific results that you can measure to show whether or not the training has been effective.

Notice that we subjected our initial ideas to a thorough scrutiny. Our initial ideas were simply that: first ideas that were a basis for further consideration. Rigorous thought and discussion with colleagues enabled us to develop and refine those initial ideas and conclude by identifying clear and specific learning outcomes.

Follow-up

With reference to a current training course you are organizing, consider and make notes on the following:

1 Who needs the training that you are thinking of?

2 What is their present level of knowledge and skills?

3 What level of knowledge and skills do you want them to be able to reach by the end of the course?

4 Are there significant difficulties in their attitude?

5 Specify the SMART learning outcomes of the training.

Tomorrow, Tuesday, we will look at how to design your course in detail, from the actual content to the provision of adequate breaks.

SUNDAY

MONDAY

TUESDAY

WEDNESDAY

THURSDAY

FRIDAY

SATURDAY

Fact-check

1. When assessing the needs of colleagues who need training you should consider:
a) Only the present level of those you want to train ❑
b) Only the final level of those you want to train ❑
c) Both the present level of those you want to train and the level you want them to be at by the end of the training ❑
d) The brand of coffee you will use at mid-morning break ❑

2. When assessing colleagues' training needs, you gather information from:
a) Only one source ❑
b) Nowhere ❑
c) Your boss ❑
d) A variety of sources ❑

3. You should discuss your thoughts on colleagues' training needs with:
a) The colleagues themselves and other colleagues ❑
b) As many people as possible ❑
c) No one: keep the matter confidential ❑
d) Only the colleagues themselves ❑

4. When considering training needs, thinking about who actually needs training is:
a) Useful if you have the time ❑
b) Unimportant ❑
c) Vital ❑
d) Something you should have thought about earlier ❑

5. Which of the following is not important when considering training needs?
a) Colleagues' skills and abilities ❑
b) Colleagues' holiday plans ❑
c) Colleagues' knowledge and experience ❑
d) Colleagues' attitude and motivation ❑

6. Learning outcomes are:
a) The content of the training course ❑
b) The results of the training ❑
c) The budget you spend on training ❑
d) The profit you make from a training course ❑

7. Learning outcomes should be relevant to the actual work of the colleagues being trained:
a) Where possible ❑
b) If you have the money ❑
c) Never ❑
d) Always, as an essential ❑

8. Learning outcomes should be SMART. S stands for:
a) Successful ❑
b) Strategic ❑
c) Specific ❑
d) Strange ❑

9. Learning outcomes should be SMART. M stands for:
a) Measurable ❑
b) Managed ❑
c) Marginal ❑
d) Motivating ❑

10. Learning outcomes should be SMART. T stands for:
a) Tactical ❑
b) Timed ❑
c) Transparent ❑
d) Turbulent ❑

SUNDAY
MONDAY
TUESDAY
WEDNESDAY
THURSDAY
FRIDAY
SATURDAY

TUESDAY

Design the course carefully

So far this week, we have looked at basic questions such as what you want to achieve in the training, what the context of the training is, the different ways in which people learn and different styles of training. We have also considered the present level of the colleagues who need training and the level you want them to have reached by the end of the training both in general terms and also in learning outcomes that are relevant to their job and as SMART (specific, measurable, agreed, realistic and timed) as possible. With all these matters in mind, you are now in a position to design the course.

Or to put things slightly differently, on Sunday and Monday we considered who needs training, and why; today and tomorrow (Wednesday) we will look at what the content of the training is and how you can deliver that training.

Today we will consider the need to continue to prepare and plan well, paying attention to your overall general aims and also details of the arrangements by:

- thinking about your major points
- ordering your major points clearly
- planning the overall timetable/schedule
- planning a strong beginning and ending.

Prepare well

You have already undertaken careful preparation on Sunday and Monday, so don't set that aside and reject that, but build on it.

Think about the major points of your training

Your analysis of training needs (Monday) has shown you the specific skills you want participants to have by the end of the course. You can now begin to think about the main points of the training.

One good way of helping you start thinking about the content of the training is to draw a spider diagram (also known as a mind map). Take a blank piece of A4 paper. Arrange it in landscape position and write the subject matter of the training in the middle. (Write a word or a few words, but not a whole sentence.) You may find it helpful to work in pencil, so you can rub out what you write if necessary.

Now write around your central word(s) the major points of the content of your training course that come to your mind. It is important not to list the ideas in order of importance; simply write them down. To begin with, you do not need to join the ideas up with lines linking connected items.

If you get stuck at any point, ask yourself the question words *why*, *how*, *what*, *who*, *when*, *where* and *how much*. These will set you thinking. The important point to notice about thinking is that, if you undertake this step, then later on when you come to filling out what you want to say, you will already know what it is you are writing about.

When I do this, I am often amazed at:

- how easy the task is: it doesn't feel like work! The ideas and concepts seem to flow naturally and spontaneously
- how valuable that piece of paper is. I have captured all (or at least some or many) of the key points. I don't want to lose that piece of paper!

For example, if I were to lead a course on giving presentations I could begin with the following basic diagram:

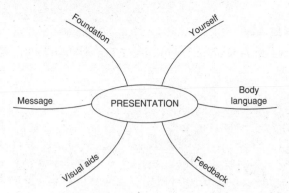

I find it helpful to add imperative (instruction) verbs:

and even to go to a third stage and add adjectives:

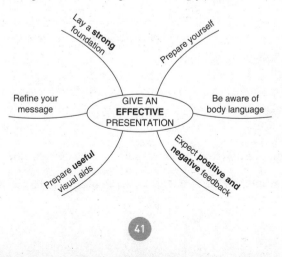

These key phrases, for example 'lay a strong foundation' and 'prepare useful visual aids', will form the key points of the main part of the training. For me, it is important that these are clearly focused: that will help them to be convincing. I have sat through too many weak, poorly argued talks and presentations.

At this point, I try to settle on the aim of the course in a maximum of 12 words. (That is the theory; in practice, it may be later in your preparation before the actual aim for that particular course becomes clear in your mind.) For my course on presentations, my aim is: 'to enable colleagues to deliver an effective presentation' (8 words). I then spend some time writing and refining my course content. Towards the end of my preparation, I ask myself whether all the content that I have planned should definitely be included. I then go back to my aim and may exclude some material because it is not central to my aims.

Order your points clearly

Particularly where much of the subject matter of the training is new to them, the participants will find it helpful if your training has a clear structure. Again, you may have sat through many presentations that have had a poor, or no, structure and you don't know where you are up to in the presentation or when the speaker will finish. So try to avoid this, and be clear and ordered.

If you can find some logical way of ordering the material, then pursue this. Examples of such logical ordering include:

● sequential or chronological
● cause and effect
● general to particular: looking at the whole then moving to a detailed analysis
● problems then solutions
● simple to complex
● listing alternatives, rejecting each one by giving reasons, until you come to the last one, which is satisfactory
● listing reasons, in order of importance

- a comparison, such as advantages and disadvantages
- similarities and differences between items.

This means that you will need to think and ask yourself, 'In order to discuss subject *y*, do I need to discuss subject *x* first?'

For example, if you are listing reasons, be clear. I find it helpful to say in the early part of a training session something like, 'We're now going to look at five different ways of...' and then I'll deliberately say, 'Firstly..., secondly..., thirdly...' and so on, as I introduce each one.

Plan a strong beginning to your presentation

Your aim here is:

- to capture the attention of your audience
- to introduce the subject
- to explain the content of your presentation
- to be interesting.

Remember you have only one attempt to make a good first impression. You are not giving an exhaustive description of everything in your introduction; you trying to attract your audience's attention and encourage them to listen attentively.

Asking questions can be useful, especially open questions (that is, ones with no fixed answer) or a closed question (that is, one with the answer 'yes' or 'no') when you know the answer will not be 'no'. In asking a question, you must do all you can to avoid evoking the answer 'So what?'

- Is it possible to be both an ethical and a successful businessperson?
- Did you know...?
- I was reading a blog yesterday...
- I was reading in today's newspaper...
- Do you want to know how...?

You could provide facts and statistics or a quotation from a well-known person.

For further discussion on beginning a training course, see Thursday.

Plan a clear end to your presentation

Work separately on the end of your presentation to round it off. Don't ramble. You could consider:

- restating the main points, summarizing them and drawing them together with reference to the aim you set out at the beginning
- reinforcing application of your main points
- relating a human interest story that explains the points you have made.

Your task is to communicate to – and maybe challenge – members of your audience on the specific next steps that you want them to take: 'So the next step is...'

An example

Let's pause in our discussion and consider an example to illustrate the points I am making.

Here is the outline of a training course for Media Associates International (MAI) that I helped lead a few years ago and which took place in a hotel in Ghana, Africa. (I am grateful to MAI for allowing me to reproduce the course programme here.)

Theme: Effective editing for clear communication

Timetable
Tuesday 23 August

8.30–9.00 am	Welcome and introductions
	Programme outline
9.00– 10.30 am	**Presentation 1: What is an editor?**
	Qualities, relevance and function of an
	effective editor
10.30–11.00 am	Mid-morning break
11.00–12.45 pm	**Presentation 2: Basic editing**
	techniques and grammar overview:
	general punctuation rules and
	application
12.45–1.45 pm	Lunch

2.00–3.30 pm	**Practical session: group work**
	Group discussion or practical
	experience
3.30 pm	Workshop assignment 1 (Homework)
	Refreshments and close

Wednesday 24 August

8.15–8.45 am	Review of Workshop assignment 1
9.00–10.30 am	**Presentation 3: Micro and macro**
	editing: detailed copy-editing and
	major restructuring of text
10.30–11.00 am	Mid-morning break
11.00–12.45 pm	**Presentation 4: Problem areas for the**
	local editor: a look at the practical
	challenges faced by the local editor
12.45–1.45 pm	Lunch
2.00–3.30 pm	**Practical session: group work**
	Group discussion or practical
	experience
3.30 pm	Workshop assignment 2 (Homework)
	Refreshments and close

Thursday 25 August

8.15–8.45 am	Review of Workshop assignment 2
9.00–10.30 am	**Presentation 5: Revising documents**
	and styling the text
10.30–11.00 am	Mid-morning break
11.00–12.45 pm	**Presentation 6: Looking beyond the**
	script: mentoring and nurturing
	writers
12.45–1.45 pm	Lunch
2.00–3.00 pm	**Presentation 7: Panel discussion: the**
	editor's publishing insights:
	A: Basic ethics of the trade
	B: Buying and selling rights
	C: Author agreements and copyright
	registration
3.30 pm	**Course conclusion**
	Evaluation (Participants)
	Refreshments and departure

Friday 26 August
Personal one-to-one consultations
10.00 am–12.00 noon
3.30–5.30 pm

The aims of the course were to develop editors' skills and increase their motivation. Specific learning outcomes included checking the structure of a text and making sure that it was written in good English, with correct grammar and punctuation.

The outline can also illustrate some of the points that we have already discussed:

- The content was spread over several sessions. We wanted to achieve a balance between instruction and motivation/ inspiration.
- The content was ordered clearly: it moved from general to particular: look at Presentation 1 (general) to Presentations 2 and 3 (specific). Such a development also applied within sessions. For instance, Presentation 1: What is an editor? consisted of the following topics:
  - *Introduction:* Since the participants were unknown to me and to some extent to one another, they introduced themselves. I asked who had received training in editing and who had not. Of the 45 present, only a few had received formal training in editing. I outlined the aims of the course and in particular (as I recall) asked participants to express what difficulties they had in editing.
  - *What is editing?*
    1 The editing process
    2 Checklist in commissioning
  - *Qualities of an effective editor:* (listing of five different qualities)
  - *Conclusion:* after summarizing the content of the session, I told the story of a newspaper editor whose identity has been forgotten although the newspaper lives on. Editors, generally speaking, do not attract attention but their work is valuable.
- The content was geared to the real needs of local (in this case, Ghanaian) editors and their work (Presentation 4).
- The content was realistic: we wanted to build on, develop, challenge and stretch colleagues' skills.
- The leading of the sessions was shared between me and three Ghanaian colleagues who were also experts in editing. I led Presentations 1, 2, 3 and 5; a Ghanaian expert led Presentation 4 and the Ghanaian organizer, who hosted the

whole training course, led Presentation 6 and all the leaders with others led Presentation 7.

- The course was interactive, meaning I involved the participants as much as I could. For example, in the first session I asked the participants to work in pairs and discuss a 'How not to edit' question that I asked, reinforcing the positive principles I had just explained.
- The course was applied. We deliberately included group discussions, practical experience and workshop assignments as integral parts of the whole course. These supported and applied the principles taught, to make sure that they were relevant to participants' needs. The assignments were then reviewed and discussed briefly at the beginning of the following days.

What else can we learn from this example?

This example also shows us:

- **The importance of breaks.** Refreshment breaks mid-morning and at lunch were built in. These allow participants time not only to assimilate and digest what had been taught to avoid information overload, but also to talk together.
- **The importance of dividing up the overall course** into sessions of an appropriate length. The course organizer

and I worked hard in our planning so that we did not put too much into each session but focused the content so that it could be assimilated relatively easily by the participants. Sessions were a maximum of 1 hour 30 minutes or 1 hour 45 minutes in length.

TIP *It is better to be ruthless before you deliver the presentation: go back to your aims and delete any material that is not essential in fulfilling those aims. Similarly, check that you have in place the content that will be necessary to fulfil the learning outcomes (as discussed on Monday).*

- **The importance of variety.** As noted above, we had a mixture of instruction from the speakers and participation by the delegates. We will discuss variety further tomorrow (Wednesday).
- **The importance of good titles.** We worked hard at these ('effective', 'challenges', 'insights') to try to make them interesting and powerful. For further help on this, see my book *1001 Words You Need to Know and Use: An A–Z of Effective Vocabulary* (Oxford University Press, 2010).
- **The importance of balance.** The combination of both instruction and motivation was appreciated by participants as being personable and inclusive.
- **The importance of being original.** In the training courses I lead I aim not only to explain the usual and expected content but also to adopt a fresh approach. So, for example, I consider not only the content of a subject but also the qualities of a person who successfully applies the content of the subject. That is why we considered the qualities of an effective editor. To apply this in a different example: I run a course on basic project management. In addition to explaining the different stages of managing a project (planning, costing, implementing), I also look at what makes a good project manager. What kind of person would they be? For example, patient, focused, a good team player. I then

ask my participants which three qualities (out of, say, 15 qualities we have listed) they already fulfil and which three they need to develop more.

Pay attention to detail

Because you are still planning the training course, you have the advantage of being able to make arrangements in advance. If you act on these during the training course, it may be too late to put matters right.

I like to think of what, firstly, I and then, secondly, all the participants will be doing at any one time (such as listening to me or discussing with a colleague or small group) and I write a list of things to do as, if it is written down, I need not keep it in my memory. For further discussion of such an overall plan, see Wednesday.

Announcements at the start of the course

I list these separately. They come before my introduction to the content of the training: I have to deal with the practical aspects early on to put participants' minds at rest about timings. This helps them feel secure in my overall leadership and direction of the day. Examples include:

- practical points: fire alarms; fire exits; location of toilets
- switching off mobile phones
- timings: breaks for mid-morning, lunch, mid-afternoon, approximate finishing time (in case any of the participants needs to leave early)
- whether you want participants to ask questions as you proceed with the training or during the time at the end of a session that you have allocated for questions.

Timings

In my preparation, I go through the planned timetable to check that there is enough time for each task. I plan the mid-morning and mid-afternoon breaks, setting aside 15–20 minutes for each. I also allow 45 or 60 minutes for lunch. On one of my courses, one of the participants said that the best thing about the day was the 45-minute lunch break, since he never usually stopped for lunch at all! For more on timings, see Wednesday.

Other practical aspects

- Producing a coursebook or handouts can be very helpful for participants so that they some material they can take home, read while travelling to and from the course, and refer to later at work.
  - If you produce a coursebook of the whole course, ensure that it is clearly structured and has a good contents page and possibly an index. The advantage of producing a coursebook is that you do not need to work through every page in detail during the course but can select those parts that are particularly relevant to your participants. Note, however, that if you are writing a coursebook, it will probably take you far longer than you think to prepare.
  - If you plan to distribute handouts, before the course collate photocopies into sets and distribute sets of papers rather than individual sheets. I made the mistake of not collating photocopies of material on the editing course discussed earlier in this chapter, so some valuable

time was lost as participants passed sheets from one to another.

- If you have handouts, consider when they will be given out: before the training session or at the end? My personal preference is before, so that the audience know where the speaker is going. The disadvantage of that is that they do know where I am going, so the notes should be a skeleton (not the full text) of the training. Make enough copies of the handouts and have some spare.

TIP *I made the mistake in one of my early training courses of preparing handouts that were in effect my full notes. So, at the end, when a colleague said, 'We didn't need really to come – we could have just read your paper,' I didn't have an answer. I learned from the experience not to reveal my whole text on the handouts!*

- Writing your own notes: the best way I have found is to take a printed copy of my handouts or coursebook and to mark in colour the headings and certain key phrases that I want to emphasize. I also make additional notes in the margin to remind me to mention certain aspects.
- Writing a lesson plan: see Wednesday.
- Check the room in which you will be training, especially all the seating arrangements.
- Know the name of a contact person on site and their phone numbers (landline and work mobile) in case of late difficulties, such as the room being locked, your being detained by circumstances beyond your control, or the projector bulb not working.
- If you are travelling by plane to a venue, send copies of your material by a secure means well in advance and take a spare copy of your material in your hand luggage (*not* in luggage for the aircraft's hold; such luggage might arrive late).
- Plan to arrive early at the venue to do a final check.

Summary

Today we have moved on from assessing participants' needs and have begun to design the content of the course. In particular, you should:

- think of the overall aim of the training course
- check that your planned content of the course will lead to the learning outcomes that you noted on Monday
- order the material so that it flows in a logical way.
- ensure that the content is:
  - *realistic*, so not too much content (or too little!)
  - *interactive*, as far as you can make it
  - *varied*: we will consider this in more detail on Wednesday
  - *fresh*, containing where possible your unique approach to the subject matter
- plan a strong beginning and end
- plan the overall timetable/schedule for the training course, ensuring you have adequate time for:
  - practical application of the principles taught that are relevant to your participants' needs
  - breaks for refreshments and so on
- plan the practical arrangements as far as you can.

Follow-up

With reference to a current training course you are organizing, consider and make notes on the following:

1 Write the overall aim of your training course in 12 words or fewer.

2 Order your material in a logical way.

3 Check that the learning outcomes you noted yesterday will be achieved by the plan you have written.

4 Write out the beginning and end.

Tomorrow, Wednesday, we'll look at how to make sure that your training course is as varied and as engaging as possible.

Fact-check

1. After you have assessed the needs of your participants and written learning outcomes, you should:
   a) Deliver the training immediately ❏
   b) Delay writing the course till you feel like it ❏
   c) Design the training course to meet those needs ❏
   d) Forget them and get on writing the course ❏

2. A spider diagram (mind map) is:
   a) A spider's web ❏
   b) A useful way to help set down your thoughts ❏
   c) A map of your brain ❏
   d) A doodle ❏

3. Participants who are learning a new subject find a clear structure to the presentation:
   a) A waste of time ❏
   b) Nice if you are that way inclined ❏
   c) To be so important that they forget the main content ❏
   d) Very helpful ❏

4. Ordering your points in your presentation is:
   a) Useful if you remember to do so ❏
   b) Very helpful as it aids learning ❏
   c) The most important aspect of your training ❏
   d) A stupid idea ❏

5. A strong beginning and end to your training are:
   a) Important ❏
   b) A luxury ❏
   c) Useful if you have time to prepare them ❏
   d) Useless – no one remembers them at all ❏

6. If you put too much information into a training course:
   a) It is a sign that you are showing off ❏
   b) Participants will not be challenged enough ❏
   c) Participants will be overloaded ❏
   d) All the participants will fall asleep ❏

7. Participants learn best if a course:
   a) Is led completely by the participants ❏
   b) Is interactive, with participation by the delegates ❏
   c) Shows no signs of clear direction or leadership ❏
   d) Is led only by one speaker ❏

8. It is _____ that the content of the course should be applied and relevant to the participants' job.
   a) Essential ❏
   b) Useful ❏
   c) Futile ❏
   d) Demoralizing ❏

9. Breaks on a training course are:
a) The only time you can check your emails ❏
b) Unproductive ❏
c) A waste of time ❏
d) Very useful to help participants assimilate and digest what they have heard and discussed ❏

10. Thinking through details of timings and practical arrangements is:
a) Unnecessary ❏
b) Useful if you remember ❏
c) Essential ❏
d) Overplanning ❏

WEDNESDAY

Plan variety creatively

We have all been on courses that have been dull and boring. The speaker begins with their PowerPoints and in the bottom right-hand corner of the slide you notice '1 of 653'. Your heart sinks as you realize you have a long, slow day in front of you!

Contrast this with a lively day, when the pace of the day varies constantly: there are times of listening to an enthusiastic speaker, opportunities for small-group discussion and even role play that everyone enjoys. You come away feeling energized and ready to put into practice what you have learned.

Today we will look at:

- the need to change the style of training throughout the course to encourage participation
- planning variety into your preparation
- preparing an overall 'lesson plan'
- different methods of training, including you as presenter speaking, illustrative stories and anecdotes, group discussion, role play and video clips
- the use of visual aids and PowerPoints.

The need for variety

I believe training sessions should be enjoyable. Participants are away from their normal jobs and (usually) want to learn. In particular, those who have been sent on the course by their bosses – and so are less motivated than those who are attending willingly – need to feel that their day is useful, enjoyable and a worthwhile experience.

I was taught to change the pace of my training every 20 minutes or so, and I always aim to do this: in other words, after about 20 minutes I endeavour to change the style in which I am trying to communicate a particular point.

Variety in teaching methods is useful for the following reasons:

- **It makes the training more interesting, motivating and enjoyable.** Using only one style, for example just listening to a speaker or solely group discussion, is boring.
- **It allows for flexibility** in case one method is not effective. If you notice that the participants are not responding during your training, you will already have planned an alternative method to communicate your point and reach your desired aim. (Your participants may or may not notice the change; that is not the point. You are simply being a good teacher and using a variety of ways to reinforce your main points.)
- **It appeals to different kinds of learner.** As we saw on Sunday, each of us has a different learning style, so one method will appeal to one person and a different method to another person. By using a range of teaching methods, you aim to appeal to different kinds of learner.

Plan variety in your preparation

In planning a training course, I sometimes write a lesson plan. This is an internal note to myself and it gives me an overview of the sessions. By preparing this I feel more in control of the training.

See the example overleaf for part of a course on Communication Skills. The notes refer to the numbered points below and are comments on the plan, not part of the plan itself.

SLIDE 1.

WELCOME

When preparing a lesson plan, consider the following points:

- Writing a plan makes you break down a large subject into small separate steps.
- You can use a plan as a basis. If discussion moves off to another point, you can decide whether to pursue that (which I often do, as it may well be more helpful to the participants than what I originally had in mind) or keep strictly to the original plan.
- The plan gives you an overall view of the training. You can see at a glance where you are at any particular point, rather than having to spend a lot of time searching through the pages of your manual.
- Inserting approximate timings in your plan makes you keep track of where you are in the session and keep a balance between the various items you want to include.
- You can add page numbers to your plan for each point in the manual so that at any given point you can say, 'Turn to page ...'
- If you are using PowerPoint slides, you can also print these out (for example at nine to a page) so you have an overview of them alongside your plan.
- Writing a plan also makes you think logically about each step:
  - Does each learning point build on the previous one logically?
  - Is there really a variety of teaching/learning methods?

TIP *For me, a lesson plan should be an overall guide. Some colleagues write out all the details; I prefer a briefer outline structure.*

Communication skills

Session number and aim	Main point; learning aims and outcomes	Subpoints	Method	Equipment needed	Timing	Notes
Session 1	Interpersonal relationships				Total 75 mins	
Aim of session: participants need to establish good rapport between colleagues; emphasize the importance of listening			Introduction: starter (to get students interested/motivated)		4	
	Develop personal qualities		Participants discuss in pairs what makes a person trustworthy (listing qualities) (5 minutes) then group feedback (7 minutes)		12	1

Notes:

1 The style that suits me is interactive learning, with discussion by participants, often in pairs or small groups, especially if you do not want to embarrass individuals by them showing their ignorance.

60

Develop good relationships with others	Ask: 1 How can you improve relationships with colleagues that you do not get on with? 2 How can you rise above office politics?	Watch video on lack of communication between colleagues (5 minutes) Questions: 1 (5 minutes); 2 (5 minutes); 3 (7 minutes); Group response (7 minutes)	Video: projector, screen	29	2
Establish rapport	How can you establish rapport?	Teaching: build on discussion so far (5 minutes)		5	3
Listening	How to become a better listener	Discussion in pairs (5 minutes) then group feedback and final thoughts (5 minutes)		10	
	Time for reflection	Individuals to consider: 'What have I learned that I can put into practice straightaway, what can I do in a couple of weeks, and what in the longer term?'		8	
	Summary	Plenary session to summarize the main teaching/learning points covered		7	

2 Notice that I have planned variety into the teaching: asking questions and watching a video. I am prepared to do both, but according to how the sessions develop I can use one or both methods.

3 Direct teaching/explanation from me, reinforcing the points participants have discussed.

Case study: Asking questions

John was new to training. He was being coached by Nigel, an experienced trainer, who encouraged John to use questions to facilitate the participants' learning. Nigel explained to John that the questions John should ask should elicit from the participants what they already knew; John could then see their level of understanding and then build on their responses. So John tested this out. For example, rather than simply teaching the good points of using email, John asked participants on his course 'What are the good and bad points of using email?'

By learning how to ask the right kinds of questions, John was able to help the participants discover more for themselves and so he became more effective as a trainer.

John also learned that good questions were open questions that began with the question words *what, how* or *why*: 'What do you think are the advantages and disadvantages of using email?' 'How can you make sure the tone of your email is appropriate?' 'Why should you never send an email when you're angry?' Later, John learned that when asking questions he should allow the participants time to answer, rather than immediately asking a further question or giving the answer himself. Participants would soon realize that the trainer was expecting them to answer the questions.

John also learned that, unless (or until) he knew a group well, he should probably not ask one of his participants a question directly. So rather than ask, 'Harry, can you tell me...?' he should direct the question to the group as a whole. Otherwise, Harry might feel unfairly treated and/or embarrassed.

Different methods of teaching/learning

You as presenter speaking

As presenter, your task for at least some of the training course will be to speak about a particular subject: you will be called on to explain a topic. Different ways in which you do this include:

- expressing the central aspects of a subject simply, at the level of your audience
- defining new terms clearly
- organizing what you are saying into a structured, logical sequence
- using vocal means well: emphasizing, repeating (by paraphrasing, for example), pausing
- using body language that is appropriate to your personality (gestures)
- communicating your message with enthusiasm
- choosing clear, appropriate and interesting examples as well as stories, quotations and facts (for more on this see below).
- summarizing the key points at the end.

I find two ways of including stories helpful: firstly, to quote good and bad examples (stories or anecdotes) from my own life and secondly to quote a story from public life, as an illustration of what I am talking about. My aim in speaking about my own life is not to boast, but to show by good and bad examples a realistic approach to the subject I am leading the course on. A well-chosen story, anecdote or quotation can strongly reinforce the point you are trying to make. It can provide a note of inspiration and increase motivation that adds energy and enthusiasm to your presentation.

Example

An important part of the successful London bid for the Olympic Games in 2005 was Lord Coe's telling of how as a young 12-year-old boy he had watched the 1968 Olympic Games and had decided he wanted to become a champion. He described how 'a window to a new world had opened to me'. It was a very simple story about being dragged into an assembly hall in his school in Sheffield. They watched the highlights of the 1968 Games, from the night or the day before, featuring local athletes from Sheffield, John and Sheila Sherwood: John won the bronze in the 400 metres hurdles, and Sheila just missed winning the gold medal in the women's long jump. Lord said, 'I just looked at this and I thought this was the most extraordinary thing I'd seen. And I was sucked in by it.' His evocative description helped London win the bid to host the 2012 Olympic Games.

The emotional effect of such a story may not always be appropriate, but in an age when we are overloaded by facts, the story of one individual can be powerful.

TIP *I recall one speaker often saying towards the end of his talks, 'Let me tell you a story' and seeing people's heads immediately rise at this phrase. Everyone loves a good story.*

All this shows us that an effective trainer will be not only someone who knows their subject well but also someone who can communicate that subject well. For me, that means thorough planning in advance and carefully selecting what I will teach. So, in my preparation I consider my aim for the overall course and each session and reject material which may be interesting but does not fit in with my aims. I then deliberately think of examples, questions and other ways in which I can communicate and explain a complex idea. And all the time, in my preparation and during the actual course, I do my best to ensure that what I am teaching is at the appropriate level of the participants.

Group discussion and exercises

Here the key points are:

- **Plan discussions or exercises in advance, before the course.** The purpose of the discussion or exercise should be to enable the participants to learn, digest and assimilate the teaching point that you have just made. For example, a training colleague of mine enjoys planning competitive games into his training to engage his participants throughout the course.

> ## Example
>
> Sometimes I suggest to participants that we negotiate what they should do but your task as trainer is always to think and suggest, or initiate, what they should do and you may negotiate the details. For example, I lead courses on project management. Towards the end of the morning session I often give the participants a task to help them realize the complexities of scheduling all the different tasks of a project. I negotiate with the colleagues on the course the nature of the actual project we will discuss in the task. It is often one relating to their work or, if the participants come from a variety of different backgrounds, then it is one that is related to a topic currently in the news.

- **Think of the purpose of the group discussion or exercise**
  Consider the following:
  - What point are you trying to communicate? Make sure that it is relevant to your overall aims. What do you want participants to grasp for themselves?
  - What exactly do you want participants to do?
  - How does this fit in with your overall plan and timing? (I recently made the mistake of beginning a major exercise too close to the end of the day.)

- How does this link in with what you are trying to teach next? Ideally, there should be a clear logical flow from one part of the training course to the next.
- **Communicate well to your participants:**
  - What exactly do you want them to do? Unless the group is very small, you will probably have to explain what you want them to do more than once, as not all the participants will be concentrating. Prepare in advance what they should do. Don't be vague or too complex. If necessary, give participants a printed explanation on a handout.
  - How long are you giving them for the task? You need to plan this well.

Example

I recently led a three-day seminar on English communication at an international university. At the end of each day, to lighten the tone of the learning experience, we held a role play. The best one was on the final day when we held a group debate on which discipline (science, social science, business) was most necessary in our current society. I divided the 18 students into four groups: three groups presenting each of these subject areas and a fourth group to chair and ask questions.

I allowed times as follows:

5 minutes: explanation

20 minutes: preparation in groups

5 minutes: introduction

3 × 10 minutes: presentation from each group

10 minutes: final discussion

5 minutes: my response to the whole session.

In actual fact, the explanation took a little less time, the group preparation took longer and the final discussion took longer as students were fully engaged. The main point is that I planned the overall timings (about 1 hour 25 minutes) in advance and allowed adequate time for the whole exercise.

- **Provide a summary at the end:** this is a brief reflection and follow-up. Often I ask the participants for their opinions before giving mine. In reporting back after discussion in small groups, I sometimes ask one of the more confident participants to come to the front and chair that session and ask the rest of the group for their feedback. Finally, I reiterate the purpose of the exercise.

Role play

In my experience, many colleagues find role play stressful. I therefore limit its use, but occasionally I use it to help reinforce learning points, and participants generally (as in the example above) enjoy it. In my courses on teaching English, I have found that the following examples work:

- an interview for a job (to practise question and answer)
- a visit to the doctor (to practise question and answer)
- a television presenter interviewing someone famous (to practise question and answer)
- a presentation to a company to persuade them to buy a product, so 'selling' a product (to practise presenting an argument)
- a presentation of various kinds, for example a decision on which place should be selected as a future World Heritage or Business Expo site (to practise presenting an argument).

> **TIP** *My general advice is: be creative; be specific (not general); prepare well.*

Video clips

Video clips, brief YouTube videos or other multimedia presentations can be very useful to reinforce the point you are trying to make. You need to spend time choosing the items well. Further, make sure that you check at the venue that any equipment works well and that the room's lighting can be dimmed (and you know where the switch is!). Make sure that the time you devote to showing videos is not too extended. Follow up the video clips with discussion that is relevant to the points you are trying to communicate.

Using visual aids and PowerPoints

Use tables and charts to support your points, but don't make these so complicated or technical that your audience cannot understand what you are trying to say. Be as simple as you can be.

Also consider using a model of something to communicate your point. For example, if you are describing the bad effects of smoking, a model that shows the effects of smoking on the lungs could have a great impact.

Use a flip chart if appropriate; I prefer a flip chart to a PowerPoint presentation as I find using a flip chart more flexible than the rigidly ordered PowerPoint. A flip chart allows you to be audience-focused and respond to points raised during interaction with members of the audience.

If you are using PowerPoint, then keep the following in mind:

● Remember that PowerPoint is a means to an end, not an end in itself. The PowerPoint should support the goal of communicating the message effectively and not be the goal itself.

- Allow plenty of time to prepare the presentation, particularly if you are not familiar with the presentation software. To begin with, it is likely to take far longer than you think.
- Don't try to put too much information on the slides. Keep to the headings, and do not write in complete sentences or give the complete outline of the talk.
- Keep to one main font. Use a large font, ideally at least 28 point. Aim to have no more than six lines per slide (have you ever peered over people's heads trying to read tiny print on a slide?). A sans-serif font is easier to read than a serif one. Headings arranged left (not centre) are easier to read; upper- and lower-case letters are also easier to read than text in all capitals.
- Work out which colours work well together, such as red on grey, yellow on blue.
- Use tables and charts to support your message; bar charts, pie charts and flow charts that give the key information visually work well.
- Use illustrations that support your message, not ones that show off your (lack of!) design or animation skills. I find that a combination of a few well-chosen words and an image that encapsulates the key idea visually works well. This can be very time-consuming, but is worth the trouble. For example, you might use a picture of buttresses supporting a cathedral to communicate the concepts of strengthening and confirming. As the saying goes, 'A picture is worth a thousand words.'
- Don't put the key information at the bottom of slides; colleagues far away from the screen may not be able to see over others' heads.
- Check the spelling or words on your slides.
- Save the presentation on a memory stick (saved in earlier versions of PowerPoint for good measure) in case the laptop fails and it has to be shown from a colleague's laptop.

TIP *If you are using PowerPoint, don't put too much information on the slides.*

Prepare ice-breakers

Ice-breakers make your participants feel relaxed and receptive to learning. On my courses I usually ask the participants to introduce themselves by giving their name, their role in their company or organization, and what benefits they would like to get out of the course. (An alternative way is to put participants in pairs, allow them a few minutes to ask the other questions and then for each participant to introduce the other person and their aims for the course.) I then write their aims on to my flip chart and even gently ask them questions to help clarify in my own mind anything about their aims that's not quite clear: it all helps set the interactive tone.

One particular ice-breaker that is sometimes used is 'Three facts': each participant has to say three facts about themselves, two of which are true and one of which is a lie. The other participants have to guess which is the lie.

In time, you will think of your own ice-breakers, but remember: don't ask someone to do what you yourself would not be comfortable doing.

Brainstorming

Here, you invite the participants to come up with lots of different ideas to solve a problem. It is important that you:

- write down all the ideas, without expressing an opinion on any of them
- allow wild ideas, which may then generate other more realistic ideas. For example, in 2004 Amazon set up a covert team to unsettle its own business; the outcome of that team's work was Kindle
- at the end, allow the group to choose which idea is best.

Keep material in reserve

With experience you will find out if you generally keep to the timings you have allocated. My experience is that I tend to underrun (that is, finish my planned material too early), so I now plan additional material in advance to use in case this occurs.

Allow time for questions

As I have indicated already this week, you should not be doing all the talking on a training course. You should plan time for questions or comments. When participants ask a question or make a comment, you can gauge the level of their understanding. During one of my early talks, I spoke non-stop for 45 minutes. In the following question time, one of the delegates asked a very basic question and I realized (too late) that my talk had been at far too deep a level for them.

In your planning and preparation, you should anticipate likely questions and prepare appropriate answers.

Keep reviewing

At the end of many of my sessions (that is, before breaks) I deliberately ask participants what they have learned in the previous session. Their thinking about this and expressing it out loud helps reinforce it in their minds.

Summary

Today has been about building on previous days' discussion of breaking down your ideas into clear, logical steps and about working out different ways of communicating effectively using a range of techniques.

In your preparation, you should:

- prepare a plan
- change the pace of your training every 20 minutes
- plan variety – a range of different ways of reaching your goal – in advance
- learn the art of asking the right kinds of question
- prepare the key message, which should be explained as clearly and as simply as possible
- think of possible stories and find relevant quotations and statistics that will support what you want to communicate
- prepare exercises: think carefully about your aims, how you will explain them to the group and the time the exercises will take
- research suitable YouTube videos you could use to communicate relevant points
- allow sufficient time to prepare PowerPoints and other visual aids to support your presentation.

Follow-up

Think of three different creative ways in which you could explain the core teaching you want to communicate.

Tomorrow, Thursday, we move from planning your training to what you actually do on the day of the course. Even here, though, preparation is key...

SUNDAY

MONDAY

TUESDAY

WEDNESDAY

THURSDAY

FRIDAY

SATURDAY

Fact-check

1. Having variety in a training course is:
a) Nice to have ❏
b) Useful if you have time to prepare ❏
c) Essential ❏
d) A waste of time ❏

2. Preparing a range of different ways of training before a training course:
a) Takes too much time, so why bother? ❏
b) Is a vital part of your preparation ❏
c) Has already been done by someone else so why not just use their material? ❏
d) Is useful but I just don't have the time ❏

3. The best questions you can ask as a trainer are:
a) Open questions that begin with 'What?' 'How?' or 'Why?' ❏
b) Closed questions ❏
c) 'When is lunch?' and 'When do we finish?' ❏
d) Ones that no one knows the answers to ❏

4. Working out how you will explain your material simply, clearly and logically:
a) Is a waste of time ❏
b) Takes far too long ❏
c) Is an important part of your preparation ❏
d) Is not one of your skills so not worth bothering with ❏

5. Using stories and anecdotes:
a) takes too much time to prepare ❏
b) Is always wrong as it deviates from the main point ❏
c) Is the only thing you do in all your presentations ❏
d) Can be helpful to avoid too much emphasis on pure facts ❏

6. Group exercises and discussions are: ❏
a) Purely a way of eeking out material ❏
b) A useful way to reinforce the points you are trying to communicate ❏
c) A waste of time ❏
d) What takes up the whole of your course ❏

7. When planning an exercise you should think of: ❏
a) What? I don't think about it at all! ❏
b) How complicated you can make it ❏
c) When it will finish so you can go home early ❏
d) What your aim is, how you will explain it and how long it will take ❏

8. You should use PowerPoint:
a) To show off your design skills ❏
b) To put all of your presentation on it ❏
c) To support the points you want to make ❏
d) You don't use it because you hate technology ❏

9. The visual aids you use are:
a) An opportunity to show off your artistic skills ❏
b) An important part of supporting what you want to teach ❏
c) So detailed and complicated that no one understands them ❏
d) A waste of time as they distract participants ❏

10. You sometimes run out of material. How do you prepare for this?
a) You prepare extra material but forget to bring it ❏
b) You stop after half a day instead of running for the whole day ❏
c) You improvise but you know it's not very good ❏
d) You prepare extra material in advance ❏

THURSDAY

Implement your plan successfully

You have completed all your preparation – you have thought about who you will train, you have analysed the skills and knowledge you want to convey and see developed in the participants, and you have written your training course, using a range of ways of communicating your message. You are now eager to start and actually put into action all that you have spent so much time preparing.

So today we look at:

- making a good first impression
- building good rapport
- starting well
- keeping the training on track
- being flexible to participants' needs
- checking that participants have understood
- using informal times well
- making sure the training is applied to participants' real situations
- ending the course well
- expecting – and so preparing for – feedback
- preparing yourself
- being aware of body language
- dealing with nervousness
- dealing with difficult people.

Making a good first impression: building a rapport

As we know, you have only one opportunity to make a first impression, so you need to make sure that the first impression you create is favourable. How can you do this? We are back to preparation:

- Arrive at the venue ideally at least an hour before the training session actually starts. This will allow you time to check the seating arrangement is as you requested, set up your laptop, the projector and PowerPoint, and so on. You will also need to double-check the location for fire exits, check whether there are planned fire drills that day, and finalize the times of breaks and arrangements for lunch. (Hopefully, arrangements for breaks and lunch will have already been made in advance.)
- Complete all your preparations before any of the participants arrive. When they start arriving, you want to spend time getting to know them and making them feel relaxed, rather than completing your set-up and your own personal preparation.

The key point here is that you want to build good rapport with the participants from the moment you first meet them. You need to work out which ways you should use to build rapport that suit your personality. I find what works for me is offering my hand to shake theirs and, as I do that, I look at them and say something like, 'Good morning. My name is Martin. I'm leading the course today.' In some cultural situations, it is not appropriate to shake hands. You will need to work out your own way of introducing yourself: what you and others in your cultural situation are comfortable with. Be yourself; be professional and friendly; be real.

 TIP *For me, the critical points are making strong eye contact and saying my name. Often, the participants will reply with their name and I can then tick their name off the list of participants that I will already have.*

I also prepare a seating plan for myself with lines for the seats; I can then add the participants' names to the appropriate seat. Obviously, if several people arrive at the same time, you may not catch all their names, but hopefully you will hear at least one of them. You can always ask, 'Sorry, I didn't catch your name.'

Generally, when participants arrive early, you can gain initial information about them. You can ask relatively easy questions about their journey and then about their workplace and role. As you talk, you may also discern whether they are excited or anxious about the course.

You should also tell the participants something about yourself, at a similar level to what they have shared. On one training course two out of the ten participants came from the town where I was born, so I was able to make a connection with them about that.

> **TIP** *The key point is that you need to build good rapport with the participants from the moment you first meet them.*

Beginning well

Mention housekeeping matters: fire exits, breaks, mobile phones off ... (see also Tuesday). Introduce yourself fairly briefly to establish your credibility in the area you will be offering training in; work out in advance what you will say about yourself. Ask participants to introduce themselves, as dealt with yesterday (Wednesday). I often make a comment here about my style being informal and interactive. My aims in saying this are to enable participants (1) to feel immediately relaxed and (2) to realize that they will not be passive listeners throughout the training course.

Your aim in this opening part is for participants to feel involved in the course from the beginning and for you to begin to discover precisely what benefits they want to get out of the course. As mentioned, you could write the participants' responses on a flip chart. This signals to them that you are serious about their particular needs, that you are willing to be flexible and that the course isn't just another course that you have delivered several times before.

After writing all the participants' expectations on the flip chart, I tear off that sheet and stick it on to a wall. Periodically, through the day I review what I have written on that sheet, to check that I am dealing with all the points satisfactorily.

Alongside listing the participants' expectations, I emphasize the key aims that I want to bring out during the training course.

At an early stage in the course I often say that what is shared in the room is confidential. Occasionally, participants mention, for example, financial details that should not be passed on to others.

As you go round the room finding out more about each participant, it may become clear that some participants have been sent on the course rather than coming of their own free will. I can think of three men from the same company who were sent on one of my courses. I needed to work hard to break through their sullenness and cynicism.

Remaining on track

One of the advantages of writing an overall session plan for yourself as described on Wednesday is that you can see where you are up to at any given point.

As also described on Wednesday, you should use a variety of different ways, such as explanation from yourself, group discussion, pair work and role play, to communicate your points.

You may notice that at some point one particular teaching method is not working or that some participants are losing interest, in which case change what you are doing and follow a different way of training, especially one that will involve them more.

TIP *Occasionally, I ask one of the more confident participants to come and lead a short session. I encourage the group to applaud that person's contribution when they have finished.*

Check participants' understanding

If you ask directly, 'Have you understood this?' the participants may nod or look at you blankly or frown. Better ways to check whether someone has understood what you have explained to them include:

- asking them to explain it to another participant
- asking them to repeat to you what you have said
- setting a task that demonstrates their understanding.

At the end of most sessions, before break, I go round the room (if numbers are below, say, 12), asking, 'What have you learned in this last session?' Some participants may just say anything, but I think it's worth it for those participants who have genuinely learned something: speaking it out loud helps reinforce it and seal it in their minds. This also gives me an opportunity to emphasize certain teaching points again.

Use informal times well

Informal times are important. Use the breaks to get to know your participants more, rather than checking your own emails or messages. Time spent gauging how the course is going (and maybe asking, 'How are you finding the course?') is valuable and can help you adjust your training as necessary.

Ensure that participants apply what you are discussing

Throughout the training course, encourage the participants to apply the points you are making to their own work situation. This should not be done in the closing minutes of the course, which is the time to *review* the learning points. It should also not be left to participants to undertake for themselves after the course. We all know that we have left a training course with good intentions to apply what we have 'learned' only to become immediately involved in the rest of life so that our good intentions are easily forgotten.

Prepare an action plan for your participants, such as the following framework:

Number	Action	Target completion date	Actual completion date
1			
2			
3			
4			
5			

Encourage participants throughout the training course to fill in the sheet: number the follow-up points, record the specific actions they need to take and note a realistic time when they think they can complete that. Obviously, they should fill in the actual completion date only when they have completed that particular action point. For example:

Number	Action	Target completion date	Actual completion date
1	See Jenny: discuss more rigorous preparation of agendas	Tuesday 3 Jan.	
2	See Mark: begin to discuss need for changes to staff appraisal forms	Thursday 19 Jan.	
3			
4			
5			

Ending well

Here, as with so much of what you have read this week, the key lies in good preparation. Expect feedback. Expect a particular colleague to raise objections because that's what they always do. Expect them... and plan for them. Deal with their objections, and where possible return to the key messages you want to communicate.

TIP *I learned a trick here: when replying to an objector, don't keep eye contact only with that person, but let your eyes roam more widely through the room. If, while you give your answer, you look only at the person raising the objection, then they may take that as an opportunity to respond even further.*

Before I started leading courses, I was afraid that participants would ask me questions that I didn't know the answers to. Acknowledging that difficulty was a first step. But I realized that I could prepare for the most common questions and, if I didn't know the answer, I could say so and offer to respond to the participants later, or in an email after the course if necessary. So if you don't know the answer to a question, be honest enough to say so. Sometimes others in the room may be able to help you out. Conclude a question-and-answer session by again positively highlighting the key message(s) you wanted to communicate to round off the whole section of your training course.

The whole training course is coming to an end. Your closing words to the participants may well remain with them. You should therefore think of some useful, strong ways you can conclude that will include a summary of your key messages and thanking the participants for coming on the course. You may also have some evaluation within the actual training (see Friday).

TIP *'Feedback' means questions from your participants, as noted earlier – and you would be wise to prepare for them.*

Preparing yourself

Some books on training devote a whole chapter to preparing yourself and dealing with nerves. In this book, my emphasis has been on making such thorough preparation that you will feel in control of as much as possible. Of course, things may still go wrong, but in your preparation you will have done all you can to minimize any potential difficulties.

Be aware of body language

A friend once told me, 'They are not listening to a message; they are listening to a messenger,' so be yourself. Look smart and then you are more likely to feel smart and more confident. Dress professionally.

When giving your training, stand up straight and relax your shoulders. Don't hide behind a lectern if there is one (although I am aware that positioning yourself there can hide your nervousness); move around the room.

Maintain good eye contact with the participants – for me, that is the critical point. If you are using a flipchart or PowerPoint, don't look at those while you are speaking; look at the participants. But look at *all* the participants, not just at those you like. Remember, too, that your whole posture will reveal a lot about yourself.

Use your voice well – speak sometimes loudly, sometimes softly, sometimes quickly, sometimes slowly. Don't mumble; speak your words clearly. Be expressive; vary the tone in which

you speak. Use hand gestures, according to your personality. Smile (in my early days of leading training courses I went so far as to write the word 'Smile' on every page of my notes). Pauses can be useful to help your audience digest what you have just said.

Prepare your message so thoroughly that it becomes part of you. Practise it by speaking it out loud. This will also help you time it.

Prepare yourself as well as your message: the important point here is to be positive: you have been asked to lead a training course, so others have confidence in you. Be as enthusiastic as possible.

In your actual training, be authentic. Sometimes at the beginning of the workshops I lead when I sense that participants and I are all nervous I will say, 'How are you feeling about today?' adding 'I'm as nervous as you.' Such genuine self-deprecating comments can help defuse any tension.

Use humour that is natural to you and appropriate to your personality and the occasion, while remaining professional.

> ## Case study: A difficult but good experience
>
> Harry was keen to improve his training skills, so his colleagues recorded a presentation that Harry gave. Harry realized that watching himself on video was a difficult but useful experience. He noticed some mannerisms he was unaware of (jangling his keys), words he kept on repeating (his recurrent one was 'OK?'). But it was worth it. The awkwardness and embarrassment he felt were a necessary part of his own learning experience. Becoming aware of his faults as others saw them was an important first step to his correcting them, as part of fulfilling his overall desire to become an even more effective trainer.

Dealing with nervousness

Almost everyone feels nervous when standing up in front of others in public. I become nervous before nearly every training course I lead and every time I have to speak in public. I have found the following helpful:

- Accept your nervousness.
- Watch out for warning signs that affect you personally, such as stomach rumbling (or worse), dry throat, shallow breathing, tension in your body, a quick heartbeat...
- Learn what works for you to reduce tension, for example sipping water, taking deep breaths, eating and drinking sensibly beforehand.
- Practise the relaxation techniques that work for you, such as walking or deep breathing.
- Make sure that you have slept adequately.
- Wear comfortable clothing that you feel at ease in.
- Practise what you will say in advance (especially the beginning and end of any formal presentation). I find practising beforehand helps me (1) realize I need to work hard choosing exactly the right words and (2) know how long the talk or presentation will last.
- Focus on your participants, not yourself. As soon as the participants begin to arrive, start talking to them. As you do this, often your own nervousness will decrease.
- Have a support group of close friends whom you can text: they can offer help and support.
- Visualize how you will feel at the end of the training course.
- Reward yourself: I find the thought of eating a bar of chocolate at the end of the course sometimes helps me through the day.

Coping with difficult people

Your aim is to remain professional and respect individuals. Here are some thoughts on how to deal with different types of people:

- **Someone who talks too much.** Say something like 'Thanks, George [without making eye contact with the participant], you're making lots of good points: I wonder if anyone else has any thoughts on this?' (and even maybe ask someone else by name for their opinion).
- **Someone who is very quiet.** As someone who was introverted for many decades, I know what this is like. A

gentle question (which you know they know the answer to, but obviously not too easy a question!) may help. Make eye contact and ask, 'What do you think, Hugh?' Praise them genuinely for their response, especially if it shows insight.

- **Someone who seems to know everything.** Ask their views occasionally; have a quiet word with them in a break so that other participants can become more involved.
- **Participants having a discussion among themselves.** Quietly go and stand near them, continuing to give your training. That will usually have the desired effect to stop them talking to one another.
- **Someone who attacks others verbally.** Ask such a person to deal with the point being discussed, not the people involved.
- **Someone who is constantly negative.** When you make a suggestion and they persist in responding, 'It'll never work,' ask them, 'Why do you say that?' Keep gently and persistently asking, 'Why?' and you may well discover some useful points. Ask such a person to suggest a positive (rather than negative) alternative to your thoughts. If they persist in offering negative suggestions, ask others in the group for their thoughts.
- **Someone who is lazy.** If the participants are working in a group, ask one of the lazy ones to report back on behalf of the group they are in. Also: ask them a question directly, 'Richard, what are your thoughts on this?'
- **Jokers.** Ignore and rise above their pettiness; remain professional, bring the discussion back to the point.

Summary

Today we have looked at the detail of leading the training on the day of the training course itself and we have discussed how to:

- make a good first impression and build good rapport
- start well
- keep the training on track, yet be flexible to participants' needs
- check that participants have understood
- use informal times well
- make sure that the training is applied to participants' real situations
- end the course well
- expect and prepare for feedback
- prepare yourself
- be aware of body language
- deal with nervousness
- deal with difficult people.

Follow-up

Consider and make notes on the following:

1 Which three points from the Summary are you good at and which three points do you need to work at harder?

2 What practical steps will you take to deal with the three points you need to work at harder?

The training session may be over but your work is not quite over. Tomorrow we will look at the important topic of evaluation.

SUNDAY

MONDAY

TUESDAY

WEDNESDAY

THURSDAY

FRIDAY

SATURDAY

Fact-check

1. Making a good first
   impression is:
   a) OK if you remember ❏
   b) Essential ❏
   c) Something not worth
      bothering with ❏
   d) Useless ❏

2. When you meet people, you
   should:
   a) Ignore them ❏
   b) Treat them with disrespect ❏
   c) Make strong eye contact
      with them ❏
   d) Look at your new shoes. ❏

3. Building good rapport with
   your participants is:
   a) Nice if you have the time ❏
   b) Useful if you are that way
      inclined ❏
   c) Vital ❏
   d) Completely irrelevant ❏

4. On a training course, you
   should:
   a) Ignore the set course and
      talk about last night's sport ❏
   b) Wander from the subject so
      much that you forget the key
      messages you are trying to
      communicate ❏
   c) Always stick absolutely
      rigidly to the course ❏
   d) Allow some freedom to
      respond to participants'
      needs, but keep within the
      overall framework ❏

5. To check that participants have
   understood something, which
   of the following should you
   not ask or do?
   a) 'Could you please
      explain that point to your
      colleague?' ❏
   b) 'Could you please
      repeat what I have just said?' ❏
   c) Set them a task that
      demonstrates their
      understanding ❏
   d) 'Have you understood
      what I just taught?' ❏

6. For you as a trainer, informal
   times are opportunities for
   you to:
   a) Check all your emails and
      text messages ❏
   b) Get to know your participants
      further ❏
   c) Move away as far as possible
      from the participants ❏
   d) Rest, as you deserve a
      relaxing break ❏

7. To make sure that
   participants apply what you
   teach them to their own
   situations, you should:
   a) Plan in application during
      the actual training course ❏
   b) Leave it to the end of the day
      if you have time ❏
   c) Hope they will work things
      out for themselves when
      they return to their jobs ❏
   d) Not apply it at all ❏

8. At the end of the course, you should:
a) Close slowly and indefinitely ❑
b) Close strongly, repeating your key messages and thanking the participants for coming ❑
c) Just leave the room to show your participants the course has finished ❑
d) End abruptly at the scheduled finishing time ❑

9. In delivering a training course you should _____ your body language:
a) Ignore or disregard ❑
b) Pay attention to ❑
c) Become so preoccupied with it that you forget your key messages ❑
d) What is 'body language' anyway? ❑

10. How should you respond to your being nervous?
a) You should become preoccupied with making sure that you don't become nervous ❑
b) You need to learn to ignore any nervousness ❑
c) You don't get nervous ❑
d) You need to learn ways to cope with nerves ❑

FRIDAY

Evaluate the training thoroughly

Well done! You have got through the day – and are just about safe and intact. Did everything go better or worse than you expected? Now is not the time to do nothing; you need to take time to evaluate – to look at how effective the training was, with the aim of making improvements and influencing future training.

You need to see evaluation as an opportunity to consolidate the content of your training and as a means of checking that effective learning has taken place.

Today we will look at:

- why you should evaluate the training
- when you should evaluate the training
- what you should evaluate in the training
- how you should evaluate the training.

Common ways of evaluating training include:

- evaluation forms
- tests
- observation
- surveys
- interviews and discussion.

It is vital that you work out how you will evaluate the training so that you ensure that all the investment made in the training has not been wasted.

Why should you evaluate?

Why should you evaluate your training? After all, isn't it enough to have dedicated yourself with a firm commitment to the training itself? Do you need to do more?

Yes, there must be more: how do you know whether all your effort was worthwhile? How do you know what the participants on your course learned? How relevant was what you tried to communicate to your participants' actual needs? What real difference is the course making to the way they work? What impact did the training have?

As we saw on Monday, evaluation is a vital step in the whole process of continuous improvement:

- **Assess:** identify training needs, for example in appraisals.
- **Plan and design:** having identified needs, you plan a training course.
- **Implement:** carry out the training course.
- **Evaluate:** review to see if the training had its desired effects; if not, reassess and begin the process again; if it has, then you can identify a further area of development to work on a different course.

Our conclusion is that you must evaluate the training in order to:

- know how effective the training has been
- ensure that the training has not been wasted
- reassess to see that your training has the desired effect.

Case study: Daring to ask the question

Joe acted as a trainer and consultant for colleagues in an engineering company who needed to write reports. He visited the company several times each year, helping colleagues write reports. After a few years he dared ask the question, 'Is my training making any difference?' The managers were surprised – but pleased – that Joe had asked the question. Answering it made the managers check that the resources they were investing were really being used effectively. They held meetings and considered the effectiveness of the training and consultancy. They concluded that Joe's time would be better spent targeting fewer colleagues who needed more attention than delivering a general course to a wider range of individuals. The overall result was a general improvement of the quality of reports – but answering Joe's question had made the managers think.

What should you evaluate?

This section builds on work by Professor Donald Kirkpatrick from the late 1950s. In *Evaluating Training Programs: The Four Levels* (1994), he distinguished four levels of evaluation:

● **Reaction**
This is the response of participants, especially immediately at the end of the training course. Participants fill in evaluation forms that ask questions about the training course's content and aims and about the trainer's effectiveness and teaching methods.

The evaluation forms provide an immediate response, especially on the extent to which participants enjoyed the course, but may not measure actual 'learning'.

● **Learning**
This is a measure of actual increased knowledge of a technique, improved skills in certain areas and changed attitudes. This can be measured by participants filling in the same questionnaire at the beginning and end of the training course, to see what changes have taken place. Responses from self-assessment forms or participants' managers, and group discussion (if the participants are all from the same company or organization) can all measure the effectiveness of learning from a training course.

● **Behaviour**
Have participants applied what was learned on the course to their behaviour in the workplace? In other words, did the training achieve a significant impact? This is best undertaken two to six months after the training course, for example by compiling questionnaires, observing the participants and through discussion with their managers. What will you measure? We are back to the specific learning

outcomes we discussed on Monday. You can see whether they have been realized and applied in the participants' actual workplace.

● **Results**

This is a measure of the effectiveness of the training on the wider business organization. One method is to measure return on investment.

> ## **Return on investment**
>
> The return on investment is the percentage return you make over a certain time as a result of undertaking the project. It is calculated according to the formula:
>
> ROI = (profits [or benefits] ÷ investment [your costs]) × 100
>
> One way of considering return on investment is to work out the *payback* period, the time taken for the profits or benefits to cover the cost of your investment.
>
> For example, a project to train all your staff in report-writing skills might cost £50,000 including the fee for tutor, materials and administration. Its benefits could be measured in terms of savings of work time and productivity increases of £60,000over one year, so the return on investment is (60,000 ÷ 50,000) × 100 = 120%.

Return on investment can sometimes be measured informally. After one of my report-writing courses with a colleague, his boss told me that it used to take him (the boss) three weeks to revise a report written by the same colleague. After my training, it took him only three days: so the saving in time and therefore financial resources was considerable.

It may, however, be difficult to measure return on investment effectively because other factors may contribute to changed results.

How should you evaluate?

We have already begun to consider different methods of evaluation today. A key point is that you should know in advance how you will use the results of the evaluation once you have received them. Ideally, they should be part of an overall continuous improvement cycle (see Monday) at both a general level within a company or organization and also at an individual level so that colleagues' personal development is monitored effectively.

Evaluation forms

Perhaps the most widely used are 'happy sheets', evaluation forms that are handed out to participants at the end of a course (or even at the end of each day if the course is longer than one day) for them to fill in before leaving. These provide information on the immediate response (Kirkpatrick's first level, 'Reaction') and also are quick to administer. They can be filled in anonymously, or with names, but may be rather subjective and will not be a measure of the longer-term learning or the overall more long-term impact of the training. At the end, results can be collated.

 Note that if you distribute evaluation forms at the end of a course and ask the participants to fill them in a few days after the course, or if you ask participants to fill in an online questionnaire a day after the course, you will receive far fewer responses than if participants have to fill one in at the end of the day of the actual course.

Here is an example of such an evaluation form:

Name .... Company .... Job title ....

Give a number on a scale of 1 = poor to 5 = excellent for the following:

1 How well did the course meet its learning objectives? ❏1 ❏2 ❏3 ❏4 ❏5

2 How well did the course meet your own learning objectives? ❏1 ❏2 ❏3 ❏4 ❏5

3 How effective was the trainer:

in their knowledge of the subject area?	❏1 ❏2 ❏3 ❏4 ❏5
in their delivery of the course?	❏1 ❏2 ❏3 ❏4 ❏5
in their understanding of the participants?	❏1 ❏2 ❏3 ❏4 ❏5
in a wide use of different methods of training?	❏1 ❏2 ❏3 ❏4 ❏5
in the pace of learning?	❏1 ❏2 ❏3 ❏4 ❏5

4 How relevant was the course to your work?
(1 least relevant, 5 most relevant) ❏1 ❏2 ❏3 ❏4 ❏5

5 Give specific examples of what you have gained from this course:
_____
_____

6 How good were the arrangements for the course (e.g. booking, travel, lunch breaks, location)? ❏1 ❏2 ❏3 ❏4 ❏5

7 What was the most useful session?
_____

Why?
_____

8 What was the least useful session?
_____

Why?
_____

9 What was your overall impression of the course?
_____

10 Would you recommend this course to colleagues? ❏ Yes ❏ No
❏ Not sure

11 Any other comments?
_____
_____

Other methods of evaluation

The following methods of evaluation are designed to measure Kirkpatrick's higher levels:

- **Tests**
  These provide an objective measure of participants' knowledge. You could administer the same set of questions at the beginning and end of the course. The questions can be multiple-choice. (I have to admit I did this once on a course and was shocked to see that most participants had given the same (wrong) answer at the beginning and end of the course to an aspect I had spent some time discussing; clearly my training was ineffective at that point.)
- **Observation**
  Some time after a course, managers or supervisors can observe the colleagues who attended the course to see whether they are in fact applying with greater confidence the knowledge and skills discussed on the course. You should use the learning needs and specific skills that were mentioned in learning outcomes (see Monday), for example on how to use certain equipment or computer software. (Obviously some colleagues will become nervous if they think they are being observed, so this needs to be taken into account.)
- **Surveys**
  These try to measure changes in attitude; that is, how colleagues think and feel about a particular subject and their motivation and perception.
- **Interviews and discussion**
  These enable the colleagues who attended a course to discuss not only their attitudes and motivation but also the ways in which the course helped them develop their skills or increase their knowledge. Interviews, in which the interviewer can gently probe the colleague for deeper responses to questions, are more time-consuming than evaluation forms but can lead to more significant results.

Note that in discussions, quieter colleagues will not talk as much as colleagues who express themselves more firmly and more often, although the quieter ones may have gained as much knowledge and developed as many skills as their more vociferous colleagues.

When should you evaluate?

We have already discussed this throughout today. To summarize, the key points are:

- Work out in advance what you will do with the evaluation you receive. Ideally, plan to include it in your overall continuous improvement programme. Evaluation is an integral part of the training, not an optional extra.
- Prepare any evaluation forms in advance of the course.
- Discuss what participants have learned before most of the breaks.
- Encourage the participants to fill in an action plan (see Thursday) throughout the course and review this at the end of the course.
- At the end of each day and especially at the end of the course, encourage participants to record in writing and, if possible, express out loud what they have learned.
- At the end of the course, fill in any evaluation sheets.
- After the course, plan to check that learning outcomes have been integrated into participants' skills, attitudes and behaviour.

Following up on a training course

Think of a training course that you have attended. After six months, how much can you remember of it? The one item I can remember from a time-management course I participated in years ago was 'Always separate planning from doing'. That takes three or four seconds to say, but I spent six hours on the course! Did I learn anything else? To be honest, I'm not sure.

One way of increasing learning and helping continuous improvement is for the trainer to follow up with the participants a few weeks after the course. The trainer could send emails or perhaps even phone the participants. (You should mention during the course that you are offering such a service.) The trainer can remind the participants what was discussed on the course. Such a reminder can serve as a prompt to jog the participants' memory and also as a check to encourage the participants to apply the training to their jobs. Participants can use the emails or other communication from the trainer as an opportunity to reflect on their experience and respond to the trainer with any difficulties they are facing. You as trainer can then reply with your thoughts on tackling the difficulties that the participants have raised.

One trainer I know systematically sends out targeted questions by email six weeks, three months and six months after a training course, and this proves an effective way of keeping in touch... and maybe helping obtain further business.

Evaluating yourself as trainer

How well do you think the training course went? You, too, should also evaluate what worked well and what didn't. What parts of the course might you need to revise if you were to lead a similar course again?

Look over your notes as soon as possible after the course has ended, while it is still fresh in your mind – that is, before your memory of the details of the course fades. Jot down thoughts on points that you would include, omit, phrase or do differently. Think which training methods worked well and which did not. Write your thoughts down, for example on your lesson plan, so that you can consider them when you next lead that course.

You may also have comments on the training venue or practical arrangements for the course. Again, note these down while the experiences are fresh in your mind.

We will look at your development as a trainer in more detail tomorrow (Saturday).

Summary

Today has been concerned with evaluating the training. We have seen that your training has not finished as soon as the course finishes.

In particular, you should:

- consider the evaluation to be an integral part of the training
- think *before* the training how the evaluation is to be used
- work out what methods of evaluation are appropriate for you
- evaluate how well the training needs and specific learning outcomes that were identified before you designed the course have been fulfilled.

Ideally, some evaluation should be undertaken as soon as possible after the training. However, if the evaluation is carried out immediately at the end of the course, then its value is limited as it will tend to be a measure of the participants' emotional responses. In order to check the longer, more lasting impact of the training you should carry out further evaluation some time after the course.

Follow-up

Consider and make notes on the following:

1 Think about when you will evaluate the training course that you are leading.

2 Think about how you have included evaluation into the overall design of your course and learning and development programme.

3 Think of three different methods you will use to evaluate the training.

Tomorrow is Saturday – we are almost there – and we will turn the spotlight on you, the trainer. How can you ensure that you keep on developing professionally and that your courses remain fresh and inspirational?

SUNDAY
MONDAY
TUESDAY
WEDNESDAY
THURSDAY
FRIDAY
SATURDAY

Fact-check

1. Evaluation is:
   a) An optional extra ❏
   b) Useful if you have nothing better to do ❏
   c) An integral part of the training ❏
   d) A complete waste of resources ❏

2. Evaluation is:
   a) Wasted ❏
   b) A way of justifying your existence as Training Manager ❏
   c) A way of checking that participants took part in the course ❏
   d) A valuable tool to help you check that the training is effective ❏

3. You need to work out what you will do with the results of your evaluation:
   a) When the results are in ❏
   b) In advance of the training ❏
   c) In the middle of the training course ❏
   d) At the end of the course ❏

4. What should you use as a basis for the training?
   a) The specific needs and learning outcomes you developed before the course ❏
   b) The participants' roles in their work ❏
   c) The inspirational and motivational aspects of your training ❏
   d) Your PowerPoint slides ❏

5. Kirkpatrick's four levels of evaluation are:
   a) Respect, Risks, Results, Return on investment ❏
   b) Reaction, Learning, Behaviour, Results ❏
   c) Behaviour, Body Language, Brands, Budgets ❏
   d) Personal, Team, Department, Organization ❏

6. An evaluation form given to participants at the end of the course is:
   a) One way of evaluating the course ❏
   b) The best way of evaluating the course ❏
   c) The only way of evaluating the course ❏
   d) The best way of checking what participants have learned and what they will apply in their work ❏

7. Pre- and post-course assessments can be used to measure:
   a) Participants' knowledge before a course ❏
   b) Participants' knowledge after a course ❏
   c) Participants' choice of food for lunch ❏
   d) Participants' knowledge before and after a course ❏

8. If you use discussion as a way of evaluating participants' assimilation of learning points after the course, you should be aware that:

a) The louder ones will be right all the time ❑

b) The quieter ones will be right all the time ❑

c) The quieter ones may talk less than louder ones but their opinions are still just as valid ❑

d) Everyone will always tell the truth ❑

9. Following up on a training course by emailing participants is:

a) A waste of time and money ❑

b) A good way to check to see what they have learned ❑

c) Useful if you have nothing better to do ❑

d) The only way to ensure they come back to you ❑

10. Which of the following should you *not* evaluate as a trainer:

a) The variety of training methods you used ❑

b) The practical arrangements of the course ❑

c) Your performance as a trainer ❑

d) The colour of the walls in the training room ❑

SATURDAY

Refine your skills constantly

Well done on coming this far! You have thoroughly prepared your training course, delivered it and evaluated it. What next?

I believe that you have begun to discover a taste for leading courses: this brief experience has increased your desire to know more.

With all this in mind, our final chapter in this book is on how to:

- review how far you have come and what you have learned
- evaluate the training: its content and methods
- identify areas you need to work on harder, for example:
  - general preparation
  - introductions
  - practical arrangements
  - increasing your confidence
  - improving rapport
  - improving listening skills
  - increasing your enthusiasm
  - ordering your material more clearly
  - being more interactive
  - being more flexible
- learn from your mistakes
- continue to prepare yourself
- further your professionalism.

By following these steps, you will equip yourself well for future training.

Review how far you have come

Throughout this book I have emphasized preparation. Prepare well at the general level: what you will say. Prepare well at the detailed level: all the practical arrangements you need to have in place for the course to go well. If one small practical arrangement goes wrong, such as a projector bulb blows or there is no water for participants, then that can have a significant effect on the whole day.

OH, AND LASTLY, MISS SMITH HAD A POINT ABOUT REFRESHMENTS

Let's review each day of this week and select some key points:

- **Know your aims in training.** What are you trying to achieve? The transfer of a body of knowledge from you as trainer to the participants – or more? Changed attitudes... changed behaviour?
- **Identify the training needs clearly.** What areas of knowledge or skills are lacking in the participants? What is the participants' starting point and where do you want them to reach by the end of the training? Identify specific learning outcomes that you can use to measure whether the training has been effective enough. In other words, *before* the training. develop some objective criteria that you can use in the evaluation later.
- **Design the course well.** Take the major learning outcomes and work out the most appropriate ways to fulfil these outcomes. Do you need to work hard at the logical ordering of your points? Again, include some evaluation of the effectiveness of the different methods of training.

- **Know your content well.** Refine it. If you are aware that your beginnings or endings are weak, spend time deliberately targeting those so that they are more effective.
- **Widen your range of training methods.** Think in advance of different approaches, games, and so on, that you can use to explain your material.
- **Practise your presentation skills.** Ask a colleague to video you. That happened to me and I immediately realized I needed to lose weight!
- **Ask a colleague to critique you.** Again, that has happened to me on a few occasions and the embarrassment is worth it: you discover personal idiosyncrasies that you are unaware of. (I tend to say, 'OK?' far too often.)
- **Have alternative plans in place in case of major difficulties.** If your laptop fails with your PowerPoint loaded on to it, work out in advance what you would do.
- **Be aware of your weaknesses in timings:**
  - If you regularly overrun, for example by spending too much time on your introduction and not leaving enough time for your main material so that you rush through that and go over your time limit, then deliberately cut out some material. You could, for instance, reduce your introduction to a bare minimum to allow sufficient time for your main points.
  - If you regularly underrun, then have some spare materials that you can use. I tend to come into this category: on a recent course I even discovered that the spare material I had prepared in advance was the most effective part of the session.
- **If you are poor at remembering people's names,** think in advance of strategies (alphabetical, pictures, stories) you can use to remember them: on a recent course I had Debra, Sharon and Tracy sitting in a row and because they were sitting in alphabetical order I could remember them that way.
- **Prepare for feedback.** Work out beforehand the outline of what you will say to likely questions.
- **Plan methods of evaluation** in advance to see how effective the training has been.
- **Identify particular areas you may need to work on harder.** For example, you have ongoing problems with

making the practical arrangements. So you could try the following:

- Make a checklist of items to check when you arrive at a venue: seating arrangements, times for refreshment and lunch, flipchart, whiteboard, laptop, name cards and/or badges, water.
- Make a checklist of items to take with you, such as Blu-Tack, highlighter pens, flipchart and whiteboard pens, spare paper (blank and ruled), pencils and pencil sharpener, ballpoint pens, eraser, stapler and staples, yellow stickies, sticking tape, scissors, memory stick with PowerPoint already loaded on.
- If you are travelling away from home, make a checklist of items to take with you, from clothes to toothpaste, spare pair of glasses, and so on.
- Update these checklists as you learn from experience.

● **Keep a file on your laptop of further subjects you may want to introduce on a course.** Recently, while leading a course on leadership, discussion turned to interpersonal relationships among colleagues at work. I was able to turn to a file on the 'Johari window' that I already had loaded on to my 'modules in training' directory on my laptop. In other words, plan to be flexible.

● **Keep up to date with industry trends.**

Learn from your mistakes

Most of the following have happened to me:

● I have arrived at a venue late, with participants waiting for me, more commonly because of circumstances beyond my control, but once when I should have ordered a taxi in advance to go to the training venue but didn't. *Lesson*: always prepare all the details of the day as far as you can.
● I have spoken at a far-deeper level than my audience: I spoke for 45 minutes (as if to Ph.D. students) and at the end one participant asked such a basic question (as if he was in a secondary school). *Lesson*: Interact with your audience *before and during* the presentation, not after it, to discover their level and direct your material at that level.

- The group lost interest in what I was trying to say; fortunately, my wife was present and, noticing what was happening, told me firmly, 'Do something!' *Lesson*: be sensitive to your audience *during* your presentation.
- I put too much of the text of my presentation on to my notes and just read those. At the end, one participant said, 'We needn't have come to hear you – we could just have read your notes.' Or I put too much information onto PowerPoints. *Lesson*: less is more.
- I spoke too quietly. At the end of the presentation, a colleague said, 'That was a lovely talk, but I couldn't hear a word of it.' *Lesson*: if necessary, use a public-address system (and add that to your checklist of items to check before a session).
- A colleague was invited to give 'a few informal thoughts on dictionary writing' but at the event discovered that it was supposed to be a formal presentation. *Lesson*: clarify in advance precisely what is expected of you.

- A colleague's microphone was left on in an informal session outside the main event and his indiscreet comments could be heard more widely than he wanted. *Lesson*: switch your microphone off outside main sessions.
- The projector failed and I couldn't use my carefully prepared PowerPoint slides. *Lesson*: have a backup plan, for example one set of photocopies of your slides which you could photocopy further at the venue.
- I hadn't prepared my material within myself enough. I had written the course several days before the course but hadn't

gone over it since then. The material I presented therefore wasn't fresh to me and my delivery lacked confidence. *Lesson*: go over your material just before you present it so that you present it in a lively and enthusiastic manner.

> **TIP** *Expect the unexpected! A colleague had to stop her course (an early refreshment break was called) for a time while she dealt with someone who had become unwell.*

Maintain your enthusiasm

I have made this a separate point because I believe enthusiasm is very important in training. I can forgive a speaker if their material is poorly structured and ordered as long as they are enthusiastic.

How can you maintain your enthusiasm?

Go over the material – but not too much. If you go over the material too much in advance of delivering it, then you may lose your freshness. So I try to spend enough time with my material until I am captivated and excited by it and feel (yes *feel*, not simply think) I have something fresh and incisive to deliver.

If you are delivering material that you have presented before, then spend time revising certain sections (for example, those that you were unhappy about on previous occasions) so that at least some of the material is new.

Read other approaches to the same subject: you will always discover new information that you can include or innovative angles you can emphasize.

> **TIP** *Go over the material until you feel passionate that you have something fresh and incisive to deliver.*

Prepare yourself

On one occasion, I was about to lead several weeks' training and to be honest I was tired even before all the courses had begun. I had prepared both the content and all the arrangements well in advance and it was the day before the first course. I found two things helpful:

1 I did something I enjoyed – looking at railways (stations, trains, timetables) and listening to classical music
2 I took inspiration from one of those quotes on a postcard you sometimes spot in a newsagent's window. I can't remember the exact words but it had a positive effect. Ones I have found helpful since include:
   - 'Go confidently in the direction of your dreams! Live the life you have imagined.' (Henry David Thoreau)
   - 'Dare to be different.'
   - 'The future depends on what we do in the present.' (Mahatma Gandhi)

On a more general note, I also keep two files to help my personal preparation:

- one containing material that may help me in training – both in terms of content and presentation
- personal notes, for example thank-you cards and emails expressing appreciation.

Develop your professionalism

Once you have begun to acquire a taste for leading training courses, you may well want to know more and refine your skills. Here are some ways you could do this:

- **Go on a public-speaking skills course.** One worldwide group that encourages this is Toastmasters International.
- **Improve your knowledge of your subject area.** Read more widely. Attend a course or even pursue a higher qualification.

- **Do you have difficulties with a particular kind of person?**
  Face up to your difficulty and discuss this with a trusted
  colleague or adviser and resolve what to do as the next step.
- **Train with a colleague.** Collaborating with a colleague will
  make you communicate explicitly about your aims, methods
  and strategies and sharpen your own skills.
- **Video yourself during an actual session.** Make yourself look
  at the video and learn to stop any unusual personal practices
  such as jangling keys, looking at a small number of people
  (not at everyone), or staring at the clock on the wall at the
  back of the room.
- **Ask a colleague to critique you.** Choose one area (for
  example low confidence, lack of rapport, not enough – or
  too much – eye contact, poor listening skills, low level of
  enthusiasm, weak structure, poor interactivity, need for
  better ice-breakers, lack of flexibility) and spend time and
  effort improving that.
- **Mentor or coach a colleague who is just setting out in
  training.** You will pass on standard lessons ('Be prepared')
  but also the invaluable lessons you have learned personally.
- **Give talks at local schools or groups.** These won't pay
  well (or at all) but you will pass on the message that is
  important to you and may inspire the next generation. I was
  first introduced to linguistics by a former pupil returning
  to my school to give a talk to sixth-form students (one of
  whom was me). His talk inspired me and changed the whole
  direction of my life.
- **Don't neglect other areas of your life.** Improve your training
  skills, but not at the expense of every other area of your life,
  including personal relationships. Know what kind of person
  you are. Nurture your inner life. Keep alive interests outside
  work that make you unique. For example, I enjoy classical
  music, so after a day with words (writing them, speaking
  them or listening to them) I enjoy relaxing by listening
  to something that does not contain words. Sometimes,
  however, the very things that stimulate us and keep us fresh
  are the things that we easily neglect when the pressure is
  on. But this is a false economy; we need to keep our own

energies flowing. Try to maintain a balance throughout different areas of your life.

- **Be determined to do your best.** Too many people settle for doing what is the minimum: the least they can get away with. We only have one life here – so do your best: excel in training.

SUNDAY

MONDAY

TUESDAY

WEDNESDAY

THURSDAY

FRIDAY

SATURDAY

Summary

Today is the last day of our week. We have come a long way this week. I hope you have enjoyed this journey with me as I have tried to encourage you to share your knowledge, skills and even your own experiences, and develop your skills as a trainer.

The emphasis today has been on:

- reviewing and evaluating different aspects of training
- identifying certain areas you could develop further
- learning from your mistakes, so you can keep improving
- maintaining your enthusiasm
- preparing yourself further
- developing your professionalism.

Follow-up

Consider and make notes on the following:

1 Do you enjoy training? Which aspects do you feel excited about?

2 Which aspect of training do you find difficult? Select one and devise an action plan to tackle this area of difficulty. Evaluate your next course in the light of this chosen aspect.

SUNDAY

MONDAY

TUESDAY

WEDNESDAY

THURSDAY

FRIDAY

SATURDAY

Fact-check

1. At the end of a training course you should:
   a) Examine in minute detail every aspect of the course ❏
   b) Evaluate the effectiveness of the training ❏
   c) Just go home and forget it ever happened ❏
   d) Think casually about it but not seriously ❏

2. Knowing your aims before you plan your training is:
   a) A waste of time ❏
   b) Useful if you remember ❏
   c) Essential ❏
   d) A luxury that no one needs to do ❏

3. Identifying specific learning outcomes before you plan your training is:
   a) A waste of time ❏
   b) Vital ❏
   c) Useful if you remember ❏
   d) Relevant only in some courses ❏

4. Having identified areas you can work hard on for the future, you should:
   a) Promptly forget them ❏
   b) Ask colleagues what their thoughts are ❏
   c) Work out an action plan to improve those skills ❏
   d) Devote every working minute in the following six months on that area ❏

5. Having made mistakes in training, you should:
   a) Learn from your mistakes ❏
   b) Lose your self-confidence and never train again ❏
   c) Repeat the same mistake ❏
   d) Keep doubting your abilities ❏

6. If your laptop fails:
   a) You have an alternative plan already in place ❏
   b) You panic ❏
   c) You hope for the best ❏
   d) It will never fail ❏

7. Maintaining enthusiasm is:
   a) Difficult, so why bother? ❏
   b) Challenging, so should be dealt with professionally ❏
   c) An unnecessary task ❏
   d) Not a problem – as you are always enthusiastic ❏

8. Checking your rapport as a trainer with the participants during the course is:
   a) Helpful if you can remember to do it ❏
   b) What is 'rapport'? ❏
   c) Not important in the slightest ❏
   d) Vital ❏

9. In your preparation for training, you need to:
a) Focus solely on your presentation and not on yourself ❑
b) Focus on neither your presentation nor yourself ❑
c) Become so immersed in your presentation that you forget to emphasize the most important things ❑
d) Focus on both your presentation and yourself ❑

10. Developing your professionalism as a trainer is:
a) A waste of time ❑
b) Important so you keep refining your skills ❑
c) Helpful if you have nothing better to do ❑
d) Unnecessary as you know it all already ❑

7 × 7

Seven key concepts

1 Identify the training need: what outcome are the participants expecting?
2 Cater for differing learning styles: everyone learns differently – ensure that you have a variety of methods in your session so that everyone gains something.
3 Remember the three learning styles and work with them: visual, auditory, kinaesthetic.
4 Continue to develop your own skills: not only as a trainer, but also to ensure that you are a guru in the subjects you run sessions about. Don't become a dinosaur!
5 Be thoughtful about the programme's design: what do you want to get across to the participants? To what degree of detail? And in what order?
6 Practise your presentation skills. To engage the participants effectively, you need to be able to communicate with them and keep them stimulated: work on your body language and style of presentation.
7 Assess your session afterwards: don't pretend difficulties didn't happen; spend some time analysing how the training went, what went well, and what you can do differently next time.

Seven questions to ask yourself

1 *Me or...?* Should you lead the training yourself, or hire an external facilitator?
2 *Why?* Why is the training needed? And why have you been appointed to organize it?
3 *How?* How will the training be conducted? And how long will it be?
4 *What?* What do you want the training to cover? What will happen after the session?

5 *Who?* Who needs the training? Is it a general session or a session covering specialized topics?

6 *When?* When will the training be held? Is it a one-off, a multi-session course or an annual refresher?

7 *Where?* Where will the training be held? On- or off-site, and what difference will this make?

Seven questions to identify training needs

1 Is a training session the best way forward, or would an open discussion forum be a better first step?

2 Do all participants carry out the same role and at the same level in the business, or will they be using their new skills in different ways?

3 What is the extent of participants' current knowledge, skills and confidence in the subject?

4 Is the training subject affected by industry trends? If so, does the trainer need to research the industry further?

5 Have any previous training sessions been run on this subject? How were they led and were they successful?

6 What is the expected outcome of this particular training session or course?

7 What is the anticipated outcome from this training in the longer term?

Seven steps to SMARTER training

1 SPECIFIC desired results.

2 MEASURABLE and quantifiable training objectives.

3 AGREED objectives with all concerned parties.

4 REALISTIC objectives that will stretch but not overload the participants.

5 TIMED to a completion date.

6 EVALUATED progress on SMART goals reviewed in future meetings.

7 REPORTED progress recorded.

Seven actions to start today

1 Create a relaxed atmosphere where participants feel comfortable asking questions.
2 Vary the pace and delivery. Do you remember the monotonous teacher's drone in the movie *Ferris Bueller's Day Off*? Don't be that teacher! Engage your audience by picking up and slowing down the pace, using visual aids, hosting Q&A sessions, and using breakout groups.
3 Listen to your participants' comments and questions – not only what they are saying, but also look for gaps based on what they are *not* saying.
4 Be flexible in your approach to training: adapt your personal style to the course you are leading.
5 Start using the training cycle: Assess and identify needs → Plan and design → Implement → Evaluate → Reassess and identify needs → Repeat.
6 Stop providing all of the answers: a good coach encourages the person to come up with solutions of their own, rather than repeating parrot-fashion what the coach has said.
7 Conquer your budget! Just like any other project you manage, make sure that the numbers add up and the training has been signed off.

Seven great quotes

1 'We are what we repeatedly do. Excellence, then, is not an act but a habit.' Aristotle (384–322 BCE), Greek philosopher
2 'Success in training the boy depends largely on the Scoutmaster's own personal example.' Robert Baden-Powell (1857–1941), founder of the Scout Movement (Of course, this quotation applies regardless of gender or age!)
3 'New people become students easily. It's maintaining that thirst for knowledge that becomes more difficult. Often it's more experienced members who put a block on their learning and they are the biggest risk to creating a winning culture.' Sir Clive Woodward, OBE, Rugby World Cup-winning England Head Coach